# JAGUAR MARK II
1955-69

A trend begins to appear—Jaguar Mark V of 1950, a classic among British sedans.

# JAGUAR MARK II

## and 240/340/S-type/Daimler V8

### plus Mark VII/VIII/IX

## 1955-69

A Documentation by Walter Zeichner

Schiffer Publishing Ltd

1469 Morstein Road, West Chester, Pennsylvania 19380

This volume of the Schiffer Automotive Series is devoted to the Jaguar Mark II. Naturally, the 2.4/3.4 Liter is included as its predecessor (later usually called "Mark I"), as are its descendants, and in reproducing historic documents the S-types are also considered, as well as some representatives of the big Mark VII, VIII and IX. This is not meant to be a guide to repairing, restoring or maintaining cars; the Schiffer Automotive Series' are rather meant to be nostalgic automobile books that take the observer back to a time that may not lie so far back, but that is already history. And those who love the classic Jaguar Mark II like to think of those days when "their" car was new.

We must not neglect to express our gratitude to the helpful collaborators who helped by making the historic documentation available, such as Andrew Whyte, Wieslaw Fusaro, Kai Jacobsen, Georg Amtmann and Robert Horender, from the last of whom comes the list of models on page 84.

Halwart Schrader
Editor

Translated from the German by Dr. Edward Force.


Library of Congress Catalog Number: 89-084166.



Printed in the United States of America.
ISBN: 0-88740-193-7
Published by Schiffer Publishing Ltd.
1469 Morstein Road, West Chester, Pennsylvania 19380

Originally published under the title "Jaguar Mk. II" 1955-69, Schrader Motor Chronik, copyright Schrader Automobil-Bücher, Handels-GmbH, München, West Germany, © 1986, ISBN:3-922617-16-6.

Please write for a free catalog.
This book may be purchased from the publisher.
Please include $2.00 postage.
Try your bookstore first.

Prewar speedster from Coventry: Jaguar SS II of 1936.

# Contents

# Jaguar Mark II—an English Classic

When one hears the imposing name of Jaguar, an auto fan thinks first of the legendary sports cars: the XK 120, XK 140 or XK 150, and perhaps too of the fabulous E-types—sports cars that, even in the age of turbo roadsters, have no need to avoid comparison with "more modern" types.

Just as popular, even if among a different breed of fans, are the Jaguar sedans. The firm founded by William Lyons in 1931—at that time it was still called SS (one S stood for *Standard,* the chassis supplier, and the other for sport)—there were always sporting sedans and coupes, such as the 2.5 and 3.5 liter cars of the early postwar era. Then the Mark V was introduced in 1948, a dynamic vehicle with a style all its own—elements of this car's styling are still found among its descendants today. At that time the car had strong competition, including the Armstrong-Siddeley, the Daimler and the 2.5 liter Riley. Then in 1955 Jaguar introduced the 2.4 Liter, which attracted attention at once—with its alluring elegance that avoided superfluous decoration and was kept quite revolutionarily smooth-surfaced. Its styling was not patterned after American standards, although the English firm's main market was then in the USA—and just for that reason the new Jaguar sold very well in the USA too. The in-line six-cylinder motor was developed from the XK series of sports cars. The displacement had been decreased in the process, for reasons of economy, coming down from 3.4 liters to 2483 cc. The power output amounted to 112 HP, sufficient for 165 kph—an attainment regarded then as quite noteworthy.

The external parts of the body were welded to a very stable frame of two longitudinally running main members with numerous transverse braces and the chassis plate, which formed the foundation for the A, B and C columns, the trunk frame and the inner fenders. With this type of self-supporting body, a high priority was given to stability, which resulted in great firmness and rigidity of the body, but also in high weight (the 2.4 Liter weighed 1230 kg empty). Particular stress was given to the long, extended lines by covering the rear wheels with so-called spats, and the interior was dominated by that inimitable mixture of leather and wood that was, in England, not restricted to the cars of the highest classes.

So the new car inspired excitement and praise at once, which resulted in, for Jaguar, high sales figures, with well over 37,000 through September of 1959. These statistics also include the cars produced since a serious fire in the spring of 1957, using the 3.4-liter motor of the Mark VIII. This family car's motor with its dual overhead camshafts produced an impressive 162 DIN HP at 5500 rpm, which led to spectacular performance for a roomy sedan. One reached 100 kph in barely 10 seconds, and only above 190 kph did the power reach its limit and keep running without any great disturbance. Nevertheless, voices were soon raised that called this powerful car a dangerous weapon in the hands of a well-meaning family man. Yet the 3.4, thanks to its high degree of comfort and the steady performance of its silky-smooth six-cylinder motor, was probably one of the least risky cars to drive. When the car was fitted with a manual four-speed transmission (overdrive and automatic transmission were available as options), it was possible to get down to 30 kph in direct drive and then accelerate strongly and without hesitation. The Americans in particular valued this elasticity, though most of the cars shipped to America were equipped with automatic transmissions.

For October of 1959 several important changes were made to the 2.4 and 3.4 liter sedans, which were called Mark II from then on. The bodywork was still basically the same, but the enlargement of the window areas by using smaller pillars made this Jaguar look considerably lighter and more modern. The rear wheels were still covered by spats with small cutout arches, as the 3.4 Liter had already been, and in the interior a more readable instrument panel and a two-spoke steering wheel with semicircular horn ring caught the eye. From now on the two previous types were called Mark I, a designation that had never officially existed. Along with the introduction of the Mark II, there was also an even stronger motor with 3.8-liter displacement and six additional horsepower, which brought it into the class of 200-kph cars. To bring this mass safely to a stop, disc brakes were now standard; they had been offered as an option since the end of 1957. Even with the performance-inhibiting Borg Warner automatic transmission, especially for the American market, such a 3.8 liter car was one of the peppiest motor vehicles of its time, and whoever liked to see it in motion could, for a modest extra price, order stylish spoked wheels; the number of spokes was decreased in the course of time to achieve better brake cooling.

Approximately 84,000 of these three very well-developed cars were built through September of 1967, without major changes except the long-overdue

**Below: Jaguar Mark VII as it looked from 1950 to 1957.**

**Right: Jaguar Mark IX, built from 1958 to 1961.**

Saloon Car Racing was popular in the Sixties, and not just in England. The similarity of the competing cars added interest to this race.

synchronizing of first gear in the autumn of 1965. A goodly number were exported, mainly to the USA.

In November of 1962 the Mark II acquired an exclusive brother known as the Daimler 2.5 V8, as Jaguar had taken over a heavily indebted neighbor, the oldest auto firm in England, and now its smooth little V8 motor was available and ideally suited to the sportily elegant Mark II. The Daimler 2.5 V8 also featured an even more exclusive decor and established the firm's tradition of adorning their most highly refined special models with the Daimler name. In the almost five years it was in production, barely 4000 of these cars left the factory, so that such a Daimler is one of the rarest versions of this series today.

While the more powerful and luxurious models were mainly sold overseas, the British market had long desired a simplified and thus more affordable version of this very useful car. Finally, in September of 1967, the Types 240 and 340 appeared, replacing the Mark II. The motors had gained a little power, and new cylinder heads achieved even softer running than before, but in terms of furnishings, strict limitations had served to keep the price down. What was a new automatic starter worth when, as of September 1966, one sat on mere imitation leather? Economy was also practiced on the Daimler; the new model was called the 250 V8 and still had genuine leather upholstery, but the hardwood dashboard and door panels had given way to synthetic materials. This model stayed in production longest, until August of 1969, and differed externally only in the somewhat different radiator grille, the lack of a springing Jaguar on the hood, and the stylized D monogram on the rear and the hubcaps. Only something over 100 left-hand-drive Daimler 250 V8 cars were built. In September of 1968 the XJ6, the Jaguar of a new generation, had been introduced.

**Above: First press photo of the Mark II with the spoked wheels with knock-off hubcaps and whitewall tires especially popular in the USA. Left: The Mark II did not look like this in everyday life, but the sedan is a sporting car after all .**

The Mark II and its closely related 240 and 340 successors now quickly became collector cars. The time did not last very long in which one could buy a used Mark II third- or fourth-hand for a very low price—and the question of spare parts (at least in England) never became a problem. Enthusiasts all over the world took to this classic, and the fondness and enthusiasm inspired by this Jaguar during its "lifetime" grew even stronger. And the Mark II had a very definite advantage over many an "oldtimer": it is a collector car that is simultaneously a very useful everyday car.

THE JAGUAR MARK VII AUTOMATIC TRANSMISSION MODEL

No clutch, no gear lever ; simply two controls—the footbrake and the accelerator—bring to you an entirely new conception of motoring pleasure from the moment you take the wheel of the Jaguar Mark VII Automatic Transmission model. For over three years the Mark VII Jaguar with Automatic Transmission by Borg Warner has been available only for export overseas where it has given the completely trouble-free service to be expected from a form of transmission of which over two million examples are in use all over the world. Now available for the home market, more and more motorists are finding in the Jaguar Automatic Transmission model a new and thrilling driving experience in which zest of driving a high efficiency car is blended with complete relaxation and freedom from fatigue.

# A Look Back to the Fifties

The market for impressive sedans was not exactly small in Great Britain. Besides the noble names of Rolls-Royce, Bentley and Daimler, there were such excellently built upper-class cars as Bristol, Austin, Riley, Wolseley, Humber and Armstrong-Siddeley. Jaguar was an outsider. But with the appearance of the Mark VII and Mark VIII the picture changed. These cars opened the way for the later Mark II—especially as exports.

Until the mid-Fifties Jaguar made exclusively heavy luxury sedans, as they appear on these pages in the form of the Mark VII and Mark VIII. The dynamic flowing lines of these cars are impressive from the outside, and the interior, equipped in the best English tradition, was not disappointing either.

*A new conception of luxury*

In every part of the world the name of Jaguar has for long been regarded as epitomising all that is best in British design and craftsmanship allied to the highest degree of luxury, but in the new Mark VIII even the high standards of the past have been surpassed. Mechanically, the Mark VIII has been raised to a new peak of performance and refinement, whilst interior appointments are of a quality normally to be found only on coachwork built to individual order by specialist coachbuilders. The cabinet work of the instrument panel, garnish rails, window surrounds and rear interior appointments is carried out in richly figured walnut carefully matched in complete sets for each individual car. Only selected skins from the best quality hides are used for the sumptuous upholstery. Built to an ideal, the luxurious Mark VIII now more than ever stamps Jaguar as being the finest car of its class in the world.

# On choosing a JAGUAR . . . . . .

One sat on highest-quality leather seats in colors that matched the car and looked at numerous walnut panels; all that created an atmosphere found only in English cars. And the car matched the house in the country . . .

## *The Mark VIII and Mark IX Saloons*

The $3\frac{1}{2}$ litre Mark Eight Jaguar Saloon is universally acclaimed as one of the most luxurious, high-performance cars ever offered as a series production model. Its interior furnishings, cabinet work, fitments and accessories are in a tradition of refinement and craftsmanship usually associated only with the art of specialist coachbuilders.

Powered by the famous 3.442 c.c. Jaguar XK twin overhead camshaft engine, the Mark Eight is available with manually operated gearbox (with or without overdrive) or with Automatic Transmission. Flush-folding occasional tables in the rear compartment, hand-finished polished walnut fittings, deep pile rugs and fine grained soft tanned leather upholstery are among the many features which impart both elegance and supreme comfort.

The Mark Nine model is equipped with a more powerful XK engine of 3.8 litre capacity and, in addition to all the features of the Mark Eight, has power steering and disc brakes.

# Breeding and Elegance—Qualities of British Classics

Even before the war a Jaguar, alias SS, exuded that sporting elegance that fascinated many automobile fans from the start. After 1945 the models grew from 1.5 liters to 2.5 and 3.5 liters and then to bigger, more stately cars; the Mark VII and Mark VIII became luxurious status symbols that never denied their sporting qualities.

The 3·4 Litre Saloon

Even after the "small" Jaguar sedans appeared, the luxury vehicles like the Mark IX (left) were still built, so as not to lose those classes of customers.

## Technical Delicacy in Conservative Dress

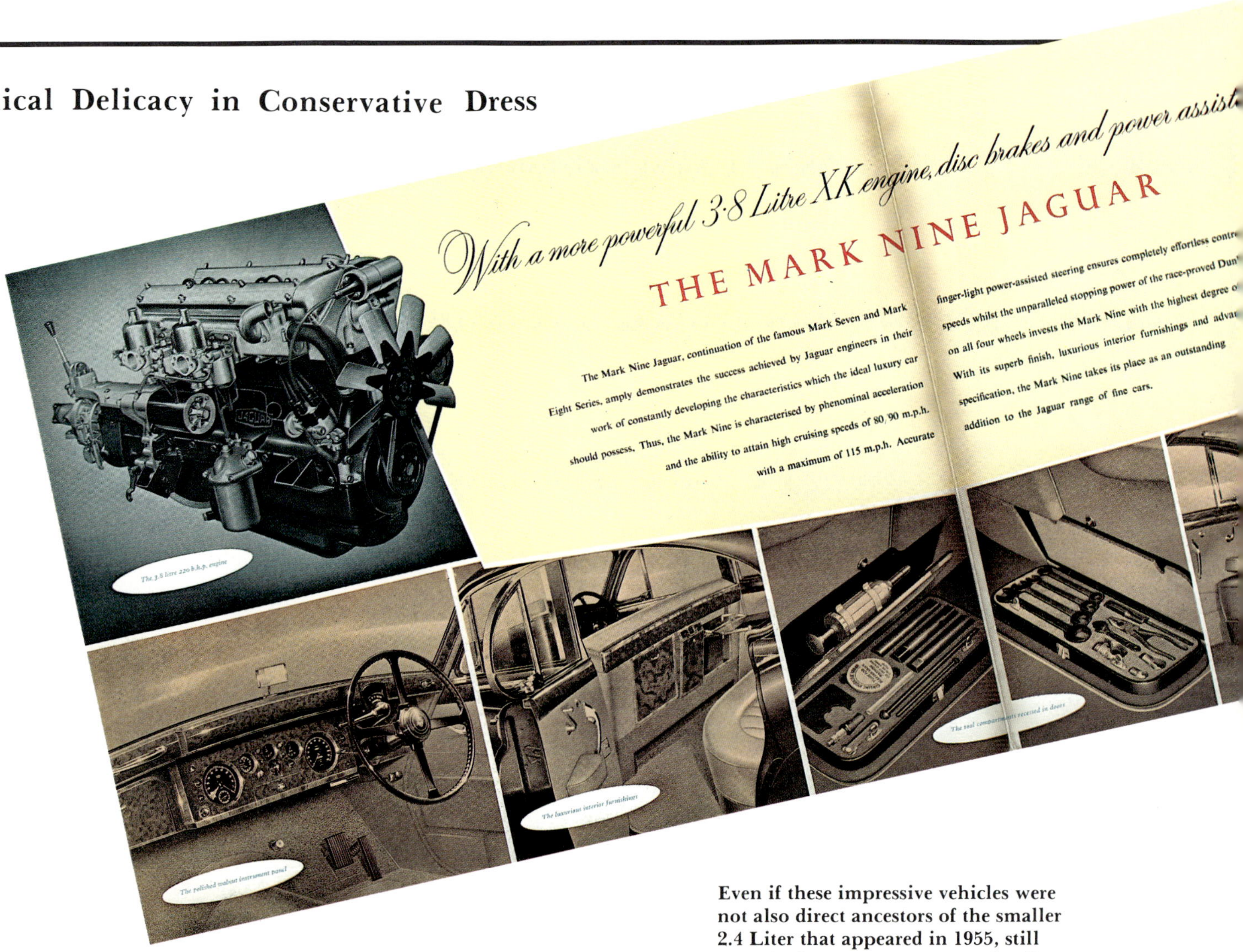


Even if these impressive vehicles were not also direct ancestors of the smaller 2.4 Liter that appeared in 1955, still even the layman can see great family resemblances, especially in the body lines with the typical form of the rear side windows and the frontal aspect.

# Jaguar Export Success, especially to the USA

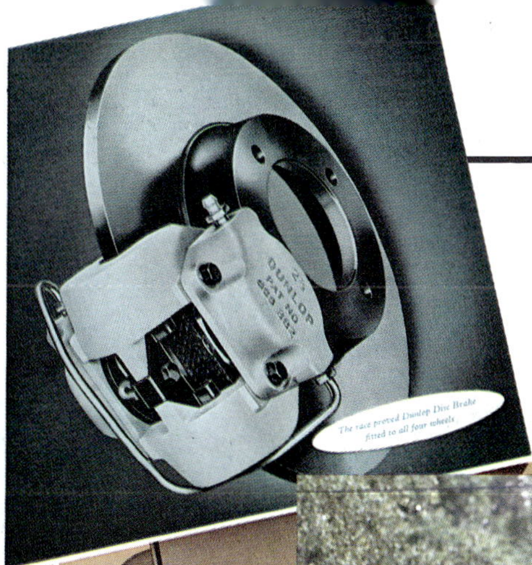

Jaguar Mark VIII, built in 1957.

Despite the somewhat conservative appearance of the Jaguar cars, up-to-date and even (as in the case of the disc brakes on all four wheels) trend-setting technology was hidden under the metal.

*The 2·4 Litre Saloon*

## *The 3.4 and 2.4 litre Saloons*

To the motorist whose personal preference is for a car of compact dimensions—the 3.4 and 2.4 litre Jaguar saloons offer all those characteristics for which Jaguar have won the highest regard the world over. Outstanding performance and phenomenal acceleration are combined with impeccable roadholding and maximum manoeuvrability at all speeds, and both models offer surprisingly economic fuel consumption.

With interior refinements and comfort in the true Jaguar tradition, the 3.4 and 2.4 saloons are available, according to type, with Manual Gearbox (with or without Overdrive) or Automatic Transmission and with Disc Brakes.

**Attracting much attention at the London Motor Show in the Autumn of 1955, was the 2.4 Liter, which introduced a new era in the history of the firm.**

The title page of an early brochure shows this new car of the rising middle class. Compared to the big sedans, this car was some 15 cm lower, 40 cm shorter, and although the wheelbase was 32 cm shorter than that of the contemporary Mark VII, there was still enough room to carry five people in comfort.

# THE 2.4 LITRE JAGUAR

Zu den bereits bekannten JAGUAR Wagen-Typen, für die der Mark VII, der Mark VIII und der XK glänzende Vorbilder waren und höchsten Weltruf gewannen, kommt jetzt der neue 2,4 Liter Wagen. Eine wunderbare Weiterentwicklung in höchster technischer und mechanischer Vollendung. Über vier Jahre haben JAGUAR Konstrukteure und Fachleute gearbeitet, um nicht nur ein völlig neues Modell herauszubringen, sondern gleichfalls eine vollkommene Neukonstruktion auf dem Weltmarkt einzuführen. Den erstaunlichen Erfolg veranschaulichen die technischen Einzelheiten und Fahrleistungen des 2,4 Liter. Die hervorragenden Eingenschaften dieses Wagens sind den vielen JAGUAR Siegen und den Erfahrungen in der harten Schule der internationalen sportlichen Veranstaltungen zu verdanken. In seiner äusseren Form fällt die wundervolle, unverkennbare JAGUAR Linienführung sofort ins Auge. Die Gesamtabmessungen des neuen Wagens sind jedoch kleiner, als die des Mark VII und Mark VIII. Trotzdem bietet das praktisch entworfene Innere des Wagens reichlich Platz für 5 Personen. Selbst der Kofferraum hat ein verhältnismässig grosses Ausmass. Demjenigen Auto-Liebhaber, der besondere Vorliebe für einen kleineren Wagen hat, wird nunmehr die Gelegenheit geboten, sich nicht nur diesen Wunsch zu erfüllen, sondern gleichfalls die Möglichkeit gegeben, Das Beste . . . einen JAGUAR . . . zu besitzen.

DAS MODELL MIT SPEZIALAUSRÜSTUNG

Along with the already famous JAGUAR car types, of which the Mark VII, Mark VIII and XK were shining examples and won the greatest worldwide renown, there now comes the new 2.4 Liter car, a wonderful new development of the highest technical and mechanical perfection. For more than four years JAGUAR constructors and specialists have worked not only to bring out a completely new model, but at the same time to place a completely new design on the world market. The astounding success is attributable to the technical details and performance of the 2.4 Liter. The outstanding qualities of this car are the result of many JAGUAR victories and experiences in the hard school of international sporting events. In its external form, the wonderful, unmistakable JAGUAR styling catches the eye. But the overall dimensions of the new car are smaller than those of the Mark VII and Mark VIII. Yet the practically designed interior of the car offers ample room for five people. Even the trunk has a comparatively large area. Those auto fans who have a special fondness for a smaller car are now not only offered the opportunity to have this wish fulfilled, but likewise given the chance to own the best . . . a JAGUAR.

Der Kofferraum ist äusserst geräumig, mit einem Inhalt von 0,38 m³. Die automatische Innenbeleuchtung erleichtert die Behandlung des Gepäcks.

Wie sein Name bereits andeutet, ist das Modell „Two-Point Four" mit einem, 2,4 Liter Motor ausgerüstet und stellt eine Weiterentwicklung des schon bekannten Sechs-Zylinder XK Motors mit zwei obenliegenden Nockenwellen und Doppel-Vergaser dar, welcher, nach dem Urteil der Fachleute der Welt, als der fortschrittlichste Motor der Neuzeit anerkannt ist. Mit einer Motorleistung von 112 PS und einem Leistungsgewicht von 9 PS/100 kg steht dem Fahrer ein aussergewöhnliches Beschleunigungsvermögen zur Verfügung, mit einer Spitzengeschwindigkeit von 160 km/Std. Diese ist mit den unnachahmlichen Eigenschaften des JAGUAR leicht und ruhig zu erreichen. In Verbindung mit diesen Vorzügen weist der Wagen die schon immer beim JAGUAR selbstverständlichen Eigenschaften, wie einzigartige Strassenlage und vortreffliche Bremsung, auf.

**THE MODEL WITH SPECIAL EQUIPMENT**

As its name already suggests, the "Two-Point-Four" model is equipped with a 2.4 liter motor and represents a further development of the well-known six-xylinder XK motor with two overhead camshafts and double carburetors, which in the judgment of the world's specialists is recognized as the most modern motor of the present time. With a power of 112 HP and a power-to-weight ration of 9 HP/100 kg, an extraordinary potential for acceleration is at the driver's disposal, with a top speed of 160 kph. This can be attained easily and quietly with the inimitable qualities of the JAGUAR. Along with these advantages, the car shows those qualities, always to be expected from JAGUAR, such as unique roadholding and excellent braking.
The luggage space is very roomy, with a volume of 0.38 cubic meter. The automatic inside light makes handling luggage easier.

The smooth lines of the new car's body in particular were very eye-catching. On the sides, the "hip curves" formerly so typical of Jaguar cars were gone, which made the car look tremendously stretched. The 2.4 liter motor with dual overhead camshafts provided ample, if not exactly breathtaking, power.

The roomy and luxurious rear seat offers the greatest possible comfort and space for 3 people. All seats are made of foam rubber and covered with aumol leather.

*Die geräumige und luxuriöse hintere Sitzbank bietet grossmöglichsten Komfort und Platz für 3 Personen. Alle Sitze sind aus Schaumgummi und mit Vaumol Leder überzogen.*

THE 6-CYLINDER 2,4 LITER JAGUAR MOTOR

DER 6-ZYLINDER 2,4 LITER JAGUAR MOTOR

# TECHNICAL DATA

**MOTOR:** 6-cylinder 2.4 liter JAGUAR motor with dual overhead camshafts, 70-degree valve angle with two-stage duplex chain drive; 83 mm bore, 76.5 mm stroke, 2483 cc displacement, producing 112 HP; compression ratio 8:1 or optionally 7:1. Two Solex downdraft carburetors, circulating-pump cooling with immersed pump with mainstream filter and floating gauze intakes in the oilpan, chrome iron engine block, tensile aluminum alloy cylinder head with hemispherical compression chambers, aluminum alloy pistons, steel connecting rods, crankshaft of 2.75-inch diameter carried in 7 steel-backed precision bearings.

**TRANSMISSION:** Four-speed single helical synchronized gears. Shift lever in center of car, mounted between the front seats. First and reverse gears 15.35:1, second gear 9.01:1, third gear 6.21:1, direct gear 4.55:1. Single-plate BORG & BECK clutch with hydraulic action; plate diameter 22.5 cm. Universal joint with HARDY SPICER gears. Hypoid differential.

**SUSPENSION:** Independent front suspension with coil springs and telescopic shock absorbers. Rear suspension by semi-elliptic leaf springs with torsion bars and telescopic shock absorbers.

**BRAKES:** Hydraulic self-adjusting Lockheed Brakemaster type brakes with servo assistance. Brake drum diameter 28.25. Brake surface 1013 square cm. Hand brake lever handily located.

**STEERING:** Burman steering with adjustable steering wheel, 43 cm diameter; optional leftor right-hand drive.

**WHEELS & TIRES:** Pressed-steel disc wheels with wide rims and "Dunlop Super-Comfort" low-pressure tires.

**FUEL SYSTEM:** Electric S.U. fuel pump. Fuel tank capacity 61.5 liters.

**ELECTRIC EQUIPMENT:** 12-volt electric system, 51 amp./hour battery. Generator with automatic regulator. Flush-fitting head- and sidelights; combined stopand taillights with built-in reflector; back-up light. Directional lights that turn off automatically, plus emergency light. Dashboard lighting. Hand-operated interior lighting. Tuned 2-tone horn. Dual two-speed windshield wipers. Starter. Automatic ignition advance with vacuum and centrifugal action. Oil coil ignition.

**INSTRUMENTS:** Speedometer of 125 mm diameter; ammeter; oil-pressure gauge, thermometer; fuel gauge with warning light.

**BODYWORK:** All-steel integral body-chassis construction for maximum rigidity; five seats; four doors; foam rubber seats with finest leather upholstery. The individual front seats are horizontally and vertically adjustable. Instrument panel and interior decorative panels of polished walnut wood. Two glove compartments. Sun visors. Soft carpeting with felt underlay. Strong wrap-around bumpers with 2 each front and rear overriders.

**TRUNK:** Large luggage space with automatic lighting.

**SPARE WHEEL & TOOLS:** Spare wheel housed in separate compartment easily accessible under luggage compartment. Tools, jack and lug wrench housed in spare-wheel compartment.

**AUTO JACK:** The jack can be applied to the body at the front or rear and used with minimum of effort.

**DIMENSIONS:** Wheelbase 2.73 meters, front track 1.39 meters, rear track 1.27 meters, overall length 4.59 meters, overall width 1.70 meters; overall height unladen 1.46 meters, ground clearance 18 cm, turning circle 10.21 meters, dry weight 1270 kg.

## The Model with Special Equipment

For all who would like to have their car especially comfortably furnished, such a model is available. It also includes a tasteful "JAGUAR" hood ornament, built-in heating, central raising armrest, windshield washing system, two independently adjustable fog lights, daily odometer, electric clock and cigarette lighter. The interior lighting works automatically when the doors are opened.



# TECHNISCHE DATEN

**MOTOR:** 6-Zylinder 2,4 Liter JAGUAR Motor mit zwei obenliegenden Nockenwellen, 70° Neigungswinkel mit zweistufigem Duplex-Rollenketten-Antrieb; 83 mm Bohrung; 76,5 mm Hub; 2483 cm³ Zylinderinhalt; Leistung 112 PS; Kompressionsverhältnis 8 : 1, oder wahlweise 7 : 1. Zwei Solex-Fallstromvergaser, Umlauf-Pumpen-Kühlung mit eingetauchter Pumpe mit Hauptstromfilter und schwimmenden Gaze-Ansaugstutzen in der Oelwanne, Zylinderblock aus Chromeisen, Zylinderkopf aus dehnbarer Aluminium-Legierung mit kugeligen Verbrennungsräumen, Kolben aus Aluminium-Legierung, Stahlpleuelstangen, Kurbelwelle von 2¾″ Durchmesser, 7-fach in grossen, mit Stahl hinterlegten Präzisions-Lagern gelagert.

**KRAFTÜBERTRAGUNG:** 4-Gang, einfach-schrägverzahntes Synchrongetriebe. Schalthebel in Wagenmitte, zwischen Vordersitzen liegend angebracht. Übersetzungsverhältnisse: Erster und Rückwartsgang 15,35 : 1; zweiter Gang 9,01 : 1; dritter Gang 6,21 : 1; direkter Gang 4,55 : 1. Einplattenkupplung BORG & BECK mit hydraulischer Betätigung; Plattendurchmesser 22,5 cm. Kardanwelle mit HARDY SPICER Gelenken. Hypoid-Hinterachse.

**RADAUFHÄNGUNG:** Vorderradaufhängung unabhängig mit Spiralfedern und Teleskop-Stossdämpfern. Hinterradaufhängung mit halbellyptischen Langfedern mit Torsionsstreben und Teleskop-Stossdämpfern.

**BREMSEN:** Hydraulische, selbsteinstellende Lockheed Bremsen Typ Brakemaster mit Servo-Bremshilfe. Bremstrommeln mit 28,25 Druchmesser. Bremsbelagfläche 1013 cm². Handbremshebel leicht zugänglich angebracht.

**STEUERUNG:** Burman-Lenkung mit verstellbarem Lenkrad 43 cm Durchmesser; wahlweise Links- oder Rechtssteuerung.

**RÄDER UND REIFEN:** Press-Stahl-Scheibenräder mit breiten Felgen und „Dunlop-Super-Komfort" Niederdruckfedern 6,40 × 15.

**TREIBSTOFFSYSTEM:** Elektrische S.U. Benzinförderpumpe. Benzintankinhalt 61,5 Liter.

**ELEKTRISCHE AUSRÜSTUNG:** Elektrische Ausrüstung mit 12-Volt System; 51 Ampèrestunden-Batterie. Dynamo mit automatischem Regler. Versenkte Scheinwerfer und Seitenlampen; kombinierte Schluss- und Stoplichter mit eingebautem Reflektor; Rückfahrlicht. Blinker mit automatischer Auslösung und Warnungslicht. Instrumentenbrett-Beleuchtung. Von Hand bedienbare Innenbeleuchtung. Abgestimmte 2-Klanghörner. Doppelter Scheibenwischer mit 2 Geschwindigkeiten. Anlasser. Automatische Zündverstellung mit Vacuum- und Fliehkraftbetätigung. Oel-Zündspule.

**INSTRUMENTE:** Tachometer 125 mm Durchmesser; Ampèremeter; Oeldruckmesser, Thermometer; Benzinuhr mit Warnungslicht.

**KAROSSERIE:** Selbsttragende, verwindungssteife Karosserie, Ganzstahl-Konstruktion; fünfplätzig; vier Türen; Schaumgummi-Sitze mit feinstem Leder überzogen. Die vorderen Einzelsitze sind horizontal und vertikal verstellbar. Instrumentenbrett und innere Zierleisten aus poliertem Walnussholz. Zwei Handschuhfächer. Sonnenblenden. Weiche Teppiche mit Filzunterlagen. Kräftige, weit herumgezogene Stosstangen mit je 2 Hornaufsätzen vorn und hinten.

**KOFFERRAUM:** Grosser Kofferraum mit automatischer Beleuchtung.

**RESERVERAD UND WERKZEUGE:** Unterbringung des Reserverades in einem separaten Fach in leicht zugänglicher Lage unter dem Kofferraum. Werkzeuge, Heber und Radmutterschlüssel sind im Reserveradraum untergebracht.

**WAGENHEBER:** Zum Radwechseln wird der Wagenheber vorn bzw. hinten an der Karosserie angebracht und kann mit geringem Kraftaufwand bedient werden.

**HAUPTABMESSUNGEN:** Radstand 2,73 m; Spur (vorn) 1,39 m; Spur hinten 1,27 m; Gesamtlänge 4,59 m; Gesamtbreite 1,70 m; Gesamthöhe unbeladen 1,46 m; Bodenfreiheit 18 cm; Wendekreis 10,21 m; Leergewicht 1,270 kg.

## Das Modell Mit Spezialausrüstung

*Für alle die ihren Wagen besonders komfortabel ausgerüstet haben möchten, ist ein derartiges Modell vorhanden. Dazu gehört eine geschmackvolle „JAGUAR" Kühlerfigur, eingebaute Heizungsanlage, mittlere auf- und abklappbare Armlehne, Windschutzscheiben-Waschanlage, zwei unabhängig verstellbare Nebellampen, Tourenzähler, sowie elektrische Uhr und Zigarrenanzünder. Die Innenbeleuchtung wird automatisch mit der Bedienung der Türen betätigt.*

Almost all customers ordered their cars with only minimally expensive special equipment. Overdrive was available as of 1956.

*With all the inherent quality of its marque*

The handsome instrument panel of the Special Equipment model.

**Classic beauty even in the small Jaguar: the hardwood instrument panel with clear centrally located instruments. The small clock was reserved for the special model. In the center of the steering-wheel knob was the flasher button, the first in a British car!**

The spacious and luxuriously appointed rear compartment permits of three passengers being carried with ease and in complete comfort. Seating is of finest Vaumol leather over Dunlopillo.

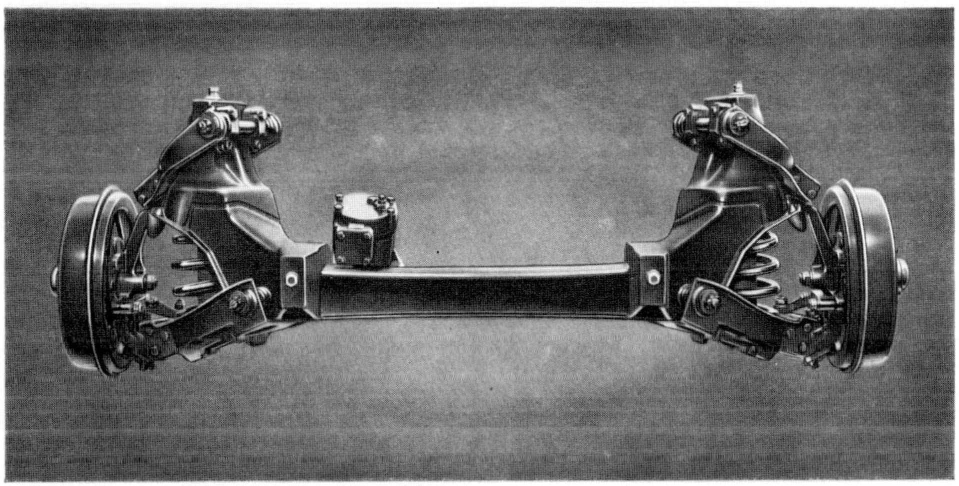

FRONT SUSPENSION SYSTEM

Contributing to the superb riding and roadholding qualities of the 2·4-litre is the front suspension system which incorporates semi-trailing wishbones and coil springs in conjunction with telescopic shock absorbers.

**The front axle construction with triangular transverse links, one above the other, and coil springs.**

STANDARD MODEL

The standard model, although fully equipped and carrying the same mechanical specification as the Special Equipment model, does not carry various items which many owners prefer either to dispense with or to add later according to their personal preferences.

MOORE'S PRESTO MOTOR WORKS, L^TD
TAMWORTH ROAD, CROYDON.

# GENERAL SPECIFICATION

**ENGINE.** Six-cylinder 2·4 litre Jaguar XK engine. 70° twin overhead camshafts driven by a two-stage roller chain. 83 mm. bore × 76·5 mm. stroke; capacity 2,483 c.c. developing 112 b.h.p. at 5,750 r.p.m. Compression ratio 8 or 7:1 (optional). Twin Solex downdraught carburetters. Cooling by pump and fan with bypass thermostat control. Forced lubrication throughout by submerged pump system incorporating a full flow filter. Chrome iron cylinder block. Cylinder head of high tensile aluminium alloy with hemispherical combustion chambers. Aluminium alloy pistons. Steel connecting rods. 2¾ in. diameter counter-weighted crankshaft carried in seven large steel backed bearings.

**TRANSMISSION.** 4-speed single helical synchromesh gearbox. Central gear change lever. Gear ratios: 1st and reverse 15·35:1. 2nd 9·01:1. 3rd 6·21:1. top 4·55:1. Borg and Beck 9-in. single dry plate clutch with hydraulic operation. Hardy Spicer propeller shaft. Hypoid rear axle.

**SUSPENSION.** Independent front suspension incorporating semi-trailing wishbones and coil springs with telescopic shock absorbers. Trailing link type rear suspension by cantilever semi-elliptic springs, radius arms and telescopic shock absorbers.

**BRAKES.** Lockheed 'Brakemaster' servo assisted self-adjusting hydraulic brakes. Brake drum diameter 11⅛ in. Friction lining area 157 sq. in. 'Pull up' handbrake mounted at floor level on the right-hand side of the driver's seat.

**STEERING.** Burman recirculating ball type steering with 17-in. diameter adjustable steering wheel. Left or right-hand steering optional.

**WHEELS AND TYRES.** Pressed steel bolt-on disc wheels with wide base rims, fitted with Dunlop 6·40 × 15-in. low pressure tyres.

**FUEL SUPPLY.** By S.U. electric pump. 13½ imperial gallon capacity tank.

**ELECTRICAL EQUIPMENT AND INSTRUMENTS.** Lucas 12-volt 51-amp./hour capacity battery with constant voltage controlled ventilated dynamo. 10-hour discharge. Flush fitting sidelamps and headlamps, integral stop/tail lamps with built-in reflectors, reversing lamps, self-cancelling flashing direction indicators with warning light, panel lights, manually controlled interior lights, twin blended-note horns, twin-blade two-speed screen wipers starter motor, vacuum and centrifugal automatic ignition advance, oil coil ignition.

**INSTRUMENTS.** 5-in. diameter speedometer, ammeter, oil pressure gauge, water temperature gauge, fuel gauge with warning light.

**BODY.** All steel full five-seater saloon. Integral body-chassis construction provides maximum rigidity with minimum weight. Four doors. Seats upholstered in finest quality leather over foam rubber cushions. Front bucket seats adjustable for height and reach. Polished walnut instrument panel and interior garnishings. Two glove compartments. Ashtrays. Interior visors. Deep pile carpets over thick felt underlay. Heavy duty wrap around bumpers with overriders at front and rear.

**LUGGAGE ACCOMMODATION.** Ample luggage accommodation is provided in a capacious rear locker fitted with an automatic light. 13½ cubic feet of luggage space available.

**SPARE WHEEL AND TOOLS.** The spare wheel is carried beneath the boot floor in a separate compartment and is readily accessible. The tools, jack and wheel brace are housed in the spare wheel compartment.

**JACKING.** Exterior jacking posts, front and rear, enable the car to be lifted with the minimum of effort by means of the jack provided.

**PRINCIPAL DIMENSIONS.** Wheelbase 8 ft. 11⅜ in. Track front 4 ft. 6⅝ in. Track rear 4 ft. 2⅛ in. Overall length 15 ft. 0¾ in., overall width 5 ft. 6¾ in., overall height 4 ft. 9½ in. Ground clearance 7 in. Turning circle 33 ft. 6 in. Dry weight 25 cwt. approx.

## *SPECIAL EQUIPMENT MODEL*

*To the motorist demanding the utmost in specification, the Special Equipment model will make instant appeal. Identified by its handsome Jaguar radiator mascot, the Special Equipment model is fitted with an interior heater and padded centre armrest in the rear compartment. Windscreen washers offer added safety, and twin foglamps, individually adjustable, are fitted. The interior lights are operated automatically by the doors, and a five-inch diameter engine revolution counter, electric clocks and cigar lighter are added to the instrument panel equipment. The already high finish of the engine is further enhanced by brilliantly polished black vitreous enamelled twin exhaust manifolds.*

*The issue of this folder does not constitute an offer and the right is reserved to alter specifications at any time without notice.*

*Printed in England by the Shenval Press, London, Hertford and Harlow*

# The Beginning of a Classic Era: The Jaguar Mark II Arrives

In 1959 the six-cylinder Two-point-four and Three-point-four types were developed into the model that went down in Jaguar automotive history as the Mark II. A car that won a great many admirers!

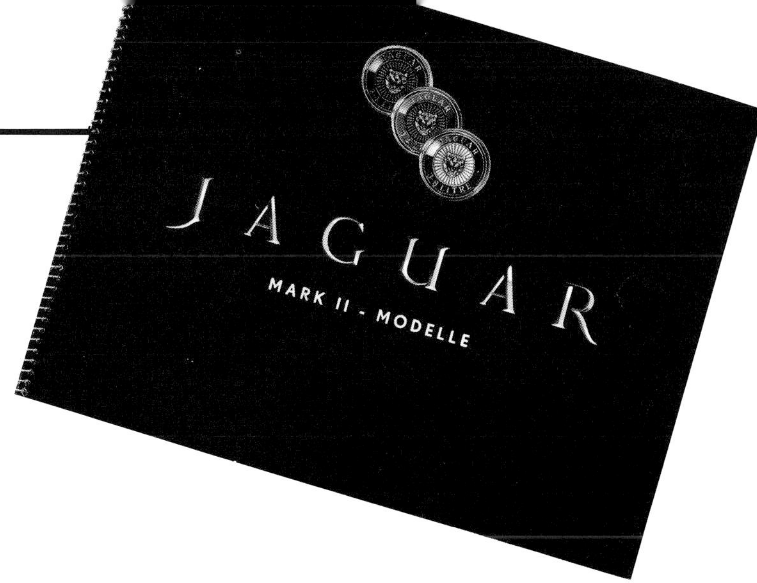


## THE NEW JAGUAR MARK II MODELS

The overwhelming success that the 2.4 and 3.4 Liter JAGUAR models have gained in all sales areas of the world have surpassed not only the bold, optimistic expectations of the JAGUAR sales department, but also the cool calculations of the engineers who had to work fast on the task of doubling production capacity in the shortest possible time. The solution of this problem was also a great success for the technicians of success, but to the great amazement of all involved, it turned out that the problem itself was not solved at all: the conditions remained as before; even today the demand far exceeds the potential for delivery!

Along with increasing the manufacturing capacity, the engineers worked intensively on the further perfection of the models then in production, and with the valuable cooperation of many JAGUAR owners there appeared the new JAGUAR MARK II 2.4, 3.4 and 3.8 liter models. Cooperation of many JAGUAR owners? Indeed. Letters from all over the world reach JAGUAR in Coventry, and their contents include the whole spectrum from enthusiastic-euphoric hymns of praise to openly expressed criticism, and they often go into detail on suggestions for improvement and express wishes and annoyances. These letters do not end up either on the mirror or in the waste basket, but in a research department formed exactly for them, where they are studied, analyzed and evaluated by trained specialists. The results of this research are then turned into calculations and drawings by the construction department, and later their results are taken up by the development and testing department.

Thus it happens that the friends of JAGUAR automobiles can see with pleasure when new models are tested that the factory has made the ideas of JAGUAR owners its own, considering and acting on them within wide parameters of possibility. The men and women who are involved in the development and construction of the JAGUAR automobile can take pride in knowing that all JAGUARs must always correspond to the driving habits and life styles of their owners, and must therefore rank high above average. Characteristic of the faultless basic concept of the JAGUAR car is the fact that that these ongoing wishes and annoyances are concerned mainly with the driving comfort, safety and amenities for the driver and passengers and only in rare cases with speed, performance, acceleration or roadholding, which in any case have been judged by public and press to be not only sufficient but extraordinarily good.

But to fulfill these individual wishes for higher top speed and even faster acceleration too, the new 3.8 Liter model appeared, and is able to satisfy the truly highest demands for performance. Where do the modifications made to the Mark II come into view? In the increased window areas overall, the slimmer pillars for the windshield and the enlarged rear window, in the super-effective disc brakes, in the easy-to-see instruments and near-at-hand controls, the heating and draftless ventilation, as well as such apparently insignificant as license plate brackets, ashtray size and location, the interior lighting of the glove compartment, the addition of a glowing cigarette lighter, and the construction and location of the brake-fluid indicator.

Just the fact that someone is seriously interested in the JAGUAR is a way of saying that the mediocre, the average has no chance, but that the highest performance is demanded in every way: perfection of the technical concept, the equipment, the quality of the materials used and the workmanship. The JAGUAR MARK II models are made to embody this "high standard". They stand at the top, alone and unequaled. They offer their owners, in all honesty, the maximum in luxury, performance and technical progress that they, according to their status in business and society, may and must demand.

JAGUAR CARS LTD COVENTRY ENGLAND

# 3.4 AND 3.8 LITER MODELS Technical Data MARK II

**MOTOR.** Special 6-cylinder 3.4 liter XK motor with B-Type cylinder head, Dual S.U. Type H.D. carburetor and dual exhaust system. Bore 83 mm, stroke 106 mm, displacement 3.442 liters. Compression ratio 8:1. Dual overhead camshafts at 70 degrees, with very high cams and two-stage roller chain drive. Water-cooling with fan, circulated by pump, thermostatically regulated. Pressure lubrication by sump-located pump and built-in mainstream oil filter. Cylinder block of chrome iron. Cylinder head of aluminum alloy with high rigidity. Hemispherical combustion chambers. Pistons of aluminum alloy. Steel connecting rods. Balanced 7-bearing crankshaft with large trunnions.

**TRANSMISSION.** (Standard). Four-speed synchronized gearbox, diagonal gearing. Shift lever located between the two front seats. Gear ratios: first and reverse gears: 11.95:1, second gear: 6.58:1, third gear: 4.54:1, fourth gear: 3.54:1. Hydraulically activated Borg & Beck single-plate clutch, 230 mm diameter, Hardy Spicer universal joint, hypoid differential.

**TRANSMISSION.** (Overdrive, fast gear). Same gears as above, but with built-in Laycock-de Normanville fast gear, which is turned on and off by a switch on the dashboard. Gear ratios: first and reverse gears: 12.73:1, second gear: 7.01:1, third gear: 4.84:1, fourth or direct gear: 3.77:1, fast gear: 2.93:1.

**TRANSMISSION.** (Automatic transmission). Automatic Borg-Warner transmission system with possibility of blocking medium gear. Gear ratios: small gear: 17.6 to 8.16:1, medium gear: 10.95 to 5.)8:1, direct gear: 3.54:1.

**SUSPENSION.** Independent front suspension with triangular wishbone transverse links, torsion stabilizer and hydraulic shock absorbers. Rear suspension with long quarter-elliptic leaf springs, longitudinal links, Panhard bar, and hydraulic shock absorbers.

**BRAKES.** Dunlop bridge-type disc brakes on all four wheels. Hydraulic action with servo assistance. "Pull-up" hand brake, floor-mounted lever, working on the rear wheels. Brake warning light.

**STEERING.** Burman ball-joint steering with adjustable steering wheel, 432 mm diameter. 4.3 revolutions from block to block. Turning circle 10.2 meters.

**WHEELS & TIRES.** Pressed steel disc wheels with lug attachment. Tubeless Dunlop 6.40 x 15 tires. Spoked wheels available optionally. Spare wheel with tire.

**FUEL SYSTEM.** By electric SU fuel pump. Tank capacity 54 liters.

**ELECTRICAL EQUIPMENT & INSTRUMENTS.** 12-volt Lucas battery, 60 amp/Hr/10 h capacity. Air-cooled generator with voltage regulator. Side lights with ruby glass insets visible to the driver. Headlights with foot dimmer switch and warning light. Separate switch for flashers. Twin fog lights. Separate stop-, tail- and directional lights in one housing. Automatically turning-off directional lights with warning light. Instrument and operating panel lighting. Indirect reading light in front. Two lights over the middle door pillars and two lights in the rear corners, switched on either manually or automatically by opening one of the four doors. Cigarette lighter with glowing socket. Tuned dual horn. Dual windshield wipers with two speeds and automatic return. Electric starter, distributor cap with automatic vacuum plus centrifugally controlled ignition. Oil-bath coil. Speedometer (127 mm diameter). Tachometer (127 mm diameter). Electric clock. Ammeter. Oil-pressure gauge. Water thermometer and fuel gauge with warning light. Combined hand-brake and brake-fluid warning light.

**BODYWORK.** Full 5-seat 4-door self-supporting all-steel safety body. Chassis and body form a unit, attaining maximal rigidity and steadiness with minimal weight. Large new arched windshield with slim pillars and new half-panorama rear window. Wide doors and arched windshield make getting in and out easier. Large rear-view mirror. All window frames chromed. Special door handles with push-buttons that cannot freeze no matter how cold. Chromed rain gutter by the vent windows. Deep foam rubber seats covered with the finest soft genuine Vaumol leather. Adjustable front seats. Front seat backs have folding tables for use by rear-seat passengers. Instrument panel of polished walnut wood with tachometer and speedometer, directly in driver's field of vision. Separate oil pressure gauge, water thermometer and fuel gauge, plus ammeter. The instrument panel includes a place for maps etc., and a locking glove compartment on the passenger's side, with interior light. An auto radio with loudspeaker can be attached under the dashboard (radio available optionally). The heating and ventilation controls are also found there, plus a very large ashtray with smoke-free ventilation.

When no radio is mounted, the aperture for it remains covered by a panel. Two-spoke steering wheel with semicircular horn ring. Front and rear doors with large pockets and armrests, the rear armrests with built-in ashtrays. Flush-fitting sun visors. Deep Moquette carpeting with thick felt underlay. Sturdy chromed wrap-around bumpers with with overiders. Chromed door handles

**HEATER & DEFROSTER.** Newly-developed JAGUAR super heater with defroster system. Separate, controllable heaters for the rear seats. Air circulation via two-speed fan, with control switch on the instrument panel.

**LUGGAGE SPACE.** Roomy locking trunk with 0.4 cubic meter capacity and automatic interior light.

**SPARE WHEEL & TOOLS.** Spare wheel readily accessible in a separate compartment under the luggage space. The tools are in a special case which, along with the auto jack and lug wrench, is housed in the same compartment as the spare wheel. (Models with spoked wheels have an additional special hammer).

**WHEEL CHANGING.** Front and rear contact points on each side of the body allow easy application of the jack and lifting of the car with minimal strength.

**MAJOR DIMENSIONS.** Wheelbase: 2.73 meters, front track: 1.40 meters, rear track: 1.36 meters, overall length: 4.59 meters, overall width: 1.69 meters, height: 1.46 meters, ground clearance: 0.18 meters, turning circle: 10.2 meters, dry weight approx. 1370 kg.

**In October of 1959 the Mark II was introduced, the furthur development of the medium—class model. The body lines were basically retained, but larger window surfaces and slimmer pillars, as well as the removal of the rear wheel spats, provided an essentially modern appearance.**

# 2,4 LITER MODELL *Technische Daten* MARK II

**MOTOR.** Sechs-Zylinder 2,4 Liter XK-Motor, zwei obenliegende, um 70° versetzte Nockenwellen mit doppelstufigem Rollen-Ketten-Antrieb. Bohrung 83 mm, Hub 76.5 mm, Zylinder-Inhalt 2,483 Liter. Leistung 112 PS bei 5750 U/min. Kompressions-Verhältnis 8:1. Doppelte Solex-Fallstrom-Vergaser. Durch Thermostat und By-Pass regulierte Wasserkühlung mit Pumpe und Ventilator. Druck-Schmierung durch im Sumpf befindliche Oelpumpe und eingebauten Hauptstrom-Oelfilter. Zylinderblock aus chromlegiertem Guss. Zylinderkopf aus Aluminium-Legierung mit hoher Festigkeit. Halbkugelförmiger Verbrennungsraum. Kolben aus Aluminium-Legierung. Stahl-Pleuelstangen. 7-fach gelagerte, ausbalancierte Kurbelwelle mit grossen Lagerzapfen von 70 mm Durchmesser.

**KRAFTÜBERTRAGUNG** (Normalgetriebe). 4-Gang-Synchron-Getriebe, schräg verzahnt, Getriebe-Schalthebel zentral zwischen den beiden Vordersitzen angeordnet. Uebersetzungs-Verhältnisse : erster und Rückwärtsgang : 14.42:1, zweiter Gang : 7.94:1, dritter Gang : 5.48:1, vierter Gang : 4.27:1. Hydraulisch betätigte Borg & Beck Einscheiben-Kupplung, 230 mm Durchmesser. Hardy-Spicer Kardanwelle. Hypoid-Hinterachse.

**KRAFTÜBERTRAGUNG** (Overdrive, Schnellgang). Gleiches Getriebe wie oben, jedoch mit eingebautem Laycock-de-Normanville Schnellgang, welcher mittels eines Schalters am Armaturenbrett zu- und ausgeschaltet wird. Uebersetzungsverhältnisse : erster und Rückwärtsgang : 15.36:1, zweiter Gang 8.46:1, dritter Gang : 5.84:1, vierter oder direkter Gang : 4.55:1, Schnellgang : 3.54:1.

**KRAFTÜBERTRAGUNG** (automatisches Getriebe). Automatisches Borg-Warner Kraftübertragungs-System mit Möglichkeit zur Sperrung des mittleren Ganges. Uebersetzungsverhältnisse: kleiner Gang : 21.2 bis 9.86:1, mittlerer Gang : 13.20 bis 6.14:1, direkter Gang : 4.27:1.

**FEDERUNG.** Unabhängige Vorderrad-Aufhängung mit Trapez-Dreieckquerlenkern, Schraubenfedern, Torsionsstabilisator und hydraulischen Stossdämpfern. Hinterrad-Aufhängung langen halbelliptischen Ausleger-Federn, Längslenkern, Panhardstab, sowie hydraulischen Stossdämpfern.

**BREMSEN.** Dunlop-Bridge-Typ Scheibenbremsen auf allen vier Rädern. Hydraulische Betätigung mit Servo-Bremshilfe. "Pull-up" Handbremse, Hebel am Fussboden montiert, auf die Hinterräder wirkend. Warnlicht für Bremse im Stand.

**LENKUNG.** "Burman" Kugel-Umlauf-Lenkung mit verstellbarem Lenkrad, 432 mm Durchmesser. 4.3 Umdrehungen von Anschlag zu Anschlag. Wendekreis 10.2 m.

**RÄDER UND BEREIFUNG.** Press-Stahl-Scheibenräder mit Bolzenbefestigung. Dunlop-Super-Ballon-Reifen 6.40 x 15. Auf Wunsch Speichenräder erhältlich. Reserverad.

**TREIBSTOFF-ZUFUHR.** Durch elektrische SU-Benzinpumpe. Tank-Inhalt 54 Liter.

**ELEKTRISCHE AUSRÜSTUNG UND INSTRUMENTE.** 12 Volt-Lucas-Batterie, Kapazität 51 Amp./St/10 h. Luftgekühlte Lichtmaschine mit Strom/Spannungsregler. Seitenlampen mit für den Führer sichtbaren Rubinglas-Einsätzen. Scheinwerfer mit Fuss-Abblendschalter und Warnlicht. Separater Hebel für Lichthupe. Zwillings-Nebellampen. Separate Stop-, Schluss- und Blinklichter in einem Gehäuse. Automatisch rückstellender Blinker mit Warnlichtern. Instrument- und Bedienungsschalter-Beleuchtung. Indirekte Leselampe im Frontabteil. Zwillingslampen über den mittleren Türpfosten und Zwillingslampen in den Ecken im Fond, welche entweder von Hand oder durch Oeffnen einer der vier Türen automatisch eingeschaltet werden. Cigaretten-Anzünder mit Leuchtsockel. Abgestimmtes Doppelhorn. Doppelte Scheibenwischer mit zwei Geschwindigkeiten und automatischer Rückstellung. Elektrischer Anlasser. Verteilerkopf mit automatischer Vacuum- sowie zentrifugal gesteuerter Zündverstellung. Oelbad-Zündspule. Geschwindigkeitsmesser (127 mm Durchmesser). Tourenzähler (127 mm Durchmesser). Elektrische Uhr. Ampèremeter. Oeldruck-Manometer. Kühlwasser-Thermometer und Benzinstands-Anzeiger mit Warnlicht. Kombiniertes Handbrems- und Bremsflüssigkeitsniveau-Warnlicht.

**KAROSSERIE.** Voll 5-plätzige, 4-türige Ganzstahl-Sicherheits-Karosserie. Chassis und Karosserie bilden ein Ganzes, wodurch maximale Festigkeit und Verwindungssteifheit bei minimalem Gewicht erreicht wird. Neue, grosse, gebogene Windschutzscheibe mit schmalen Pfosten und neuer Halb-Panorama-Rückscheibe gewährleisten maximale Rundsicht. Dank breiter Türen und gebogener Windschutzscheibe leichter Ein- leichter Ein- und Ausstieg. Grosser Rückspiegel. Alle Fenster- und Türrahmen sind verchromt. Spezial-Türgriffe mit Druckknöpfen, welche auch bei grosser Kälte nicht einfrieren können. Verchromte Tropfrinnen bei den Ventilationsflügeln. Tiefe Schaumgummi-Polsterung, welche mit feinstem, echtem, weichem Vaumol-Leder überzogen ist. Verstellbare Vordersitze. In den Rücklehnen derselben sind Klapptische eingebaut, die von den Fondpassagieren benützt werden können. Instrumentenbrett aus poliertem Nussbaumholz mit Tourenzähler und Geschwindigkeitsmesser direkt im Blickfeld des Fahrers angeordnet. Separate Oeldruck-, Kühlwassertemperatur- und Treibstoffstand-Anzeiger, sowie Ampèremeter. Das Instrumentenbrett enthält ein Fach für Karten etc. und auf der Mitfahrerseite ein weiteres verschliessbares Fach mit Innenlicht. Unter dem Instrumentenbrett besteht Einbaumöglichkeit für einen Autoradio mit Lautsprecher. (Radio gegen Aufpreis lieferbar). Ferner befindet sich dort die Heizung und Belüftung, sowie ein sehr grosser rauchfreier Aschenbecher. Wenn kein Radio montiert wird, bleibt die Oeffnung mit einer Blende abgedeckt. Zweispeichen-Lenkrad mit halbrundem Signalring. Vorder- und Hintertüren mit grossen Taschen und Armstützen, in welchen bei den Hintertüren auch Aschenbecher eingebaut sind. Grosse aufklappbare Armstützen in der Rücklehne der Fondsitze. Flush-fitting Sonnenblenden. Schwere Moquette-Teppiche mit dicker Filzunterlage. Starke, um die Karosserie herumgezogene verchromte Stoss-Stangen mit Hörnern. Verchromte Türschlösser.

**HEIZUNG UND DEFROSTER-ANLAGE.** Neu entwickelte JAGUAR-Super-Heizung mit Defroster-Anlage, wobei die Heizung für Vorder- und Hintersitze separat reguliert werden kann. Luftzirkulation durch Ventilator mit zwei Geschwindigkeiten, regulierbar am Instrumentenbrett.

**KOFFERRAUM.** Geräumiger, abschliessbarer Kofferraum mit 0,4 m3 Inhalt und automatisch einschaltender Innenbeleuchtung.

**RESERVERAD UND WERKZEUG.** Reserverad leicht zugänglich in einem separaten Abteil unter dem Kofferboden untergebracht. Die Werkzeuge sind in einem speziellen Kasten eingeordnet, welcher sich zusammen mit dem Wagenheber und Radmutter-Schlüssel im gleichen Abteil befindet wie das Reserverad. (Bei Modellen mit Speichenrädern zusätzlich spezieller Hammer).

**RADWECHSEL.** Hinten und vorn beidseitig der Karosserie vorgesehene Halter erlauben das leichte Anbringen des Wagenhebers und das Hochheben des Wagens mit minimalem Kraftaufwand.

**HAUPTABMESSUNGEN.** Radstand : 2.73 m, Spur vorne : 1.40 m, Spur hinten 1.36 m, Länge über alles : 4.59 m, Breite über alles : 1.69 m, Höhe : 1.46 m, Bodenfreiheit : 0,18 m, Wendekreis 10.2 m, Leergewicht ca. 1320 kg.

**MODELL MITT SPEZIAL-AUSRÜSTUNG.** *Der 2.4 Liter "Spezial-Ausrüstung" wird geliefert mit Heizung- und Defroster-Anlage, versenkbare Armstützen in der Mitte der Rücklehne, Scheibenwaschanlage, doppelte Nebellampen, durch Oeffnen einer Türe betätigte Innenbeleuchtung, Tourenzähler mit elektrischer Uhr, Cigarettenanzünder, emailliertes Auspuff-Sammelrohr.*

**MODEL WITH SPECIAL EQUIPMENT.**
The 2.4 Liter "Special Equipment" version is delivered with heating and defroster system, lowering armrests in the middle of the back seat, windshield washer system, dual fog lights, interior light activated by opening one door, tachometer with electric clock, cigarette lighter, enameled exhaust pipe.

Text is same as page 26 except for small item at bottom.

A more stylish environment for the Mark II than this English country house can scarcely be imagined. This is the version with the smallest motor: 2.4 liter displacement and 112 horsepower.

The newly designed dashboard with the modern two-spoke steering wheel.

## HARMONY OF PRACTICAL VISIBILITY AND REFINED BEAUTY

**Instruments and control switches**

1. Overdrive switch.
2. Choke (only in the 2.4 liter model).
3. Tachometer.
4. Speedometer with odometer.
5. Electric clock.
6. Water thermometer.
7. Oil pressure gauge.
8. Outside light switch.
9. Fuel gauge.
10. Ammeter.
11. Automatic drive switches.
12. Electric windshield washer control.
13. Electric windshield wiper control.
14. Map reading light.
15. Starter button.
16. Cigarette lighter.
17. Ignition lock.
18. Heater vent.
19. Dashboard light switch.
20. Interior light switch.
21. Automatic drive lever.
22. Daily odometer control.
23. Horn ring.
24. High beam switch.
25. Clock control.
26. Directional light control.
27. Air vent lever.
28. Heater control.
29. Radio control.
30. Radio control.
31. Heater (airstream regulator).
32. Smoke-free ashtray.
33. Brake fluid indicator.

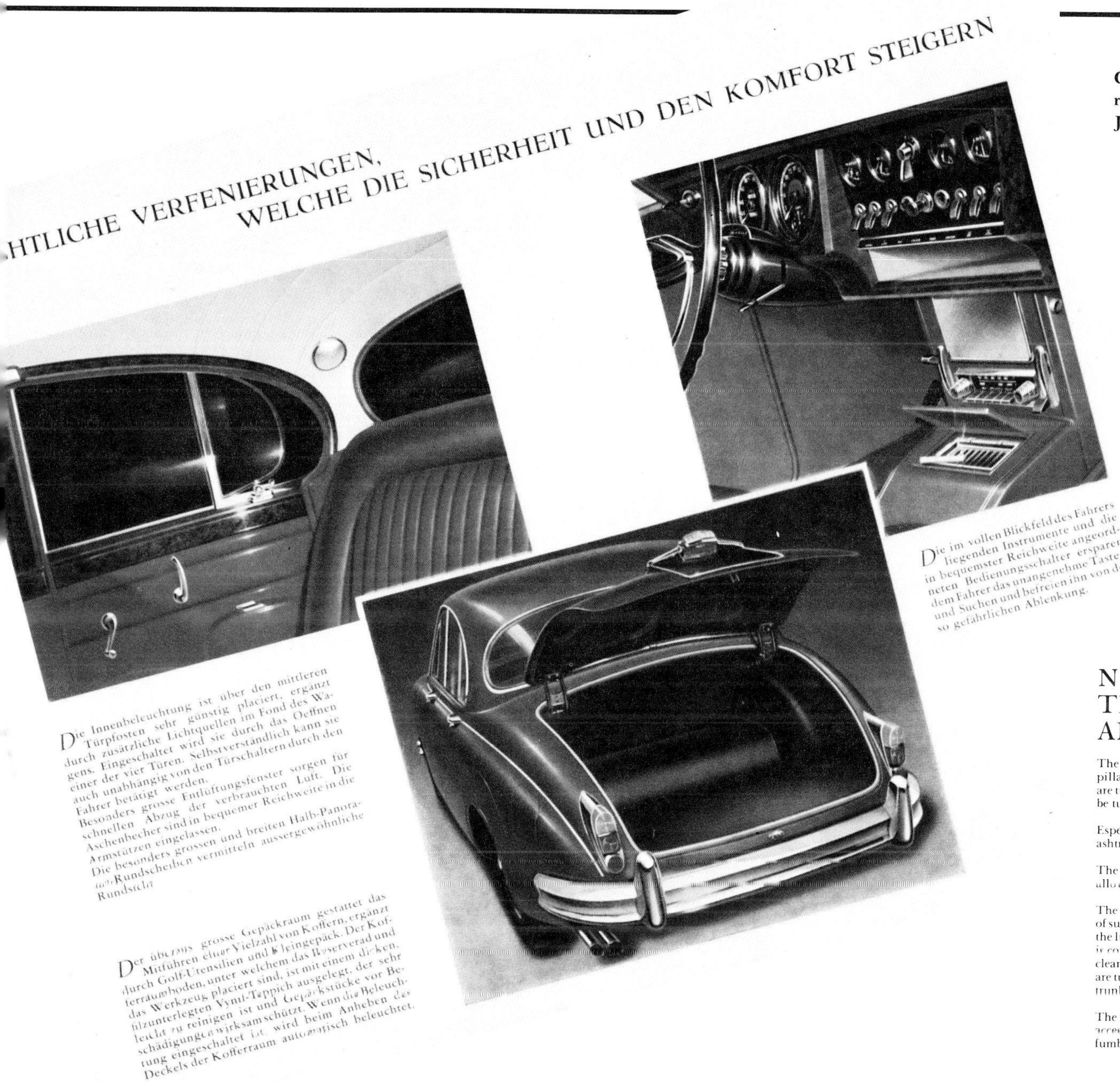

HTLICHE VERFENIERUNGEN,
WELCHE DIE SICHERHEIT UND DEN KOMFORT STEIGERN

Die Innenbeleuchtung ist über den mittleren Türpfosten sehr günstig placiert, ergänzt durch zusätzliche Lichtquellen im Fond des Wagens. Eingeschaltet wird sie durch das Oeffnen einer der vier Türen. Selbstverständlich kann sie auch unabhängig von den Türschaltern durch den Fahrer betätigt werden.

Besonders grosse Entlüftungsfenster sorgen für schnellen Abzug der verbrauchten Luft. Die Aschenbecher sind in bequemer Reichweite in die Armstützen eingelassen.

Die besonders grossen und breiten Halb-Panorama-Rundscheiben vermitteln aussergewöhnliche Rundsicht.

Der überaus grosse Gepäckraum gestattet das Mitführen einer Vielzahl von Koffern, ergänzt durch Golf-Utensilien und Kleingepäck. Der Kofferraumboden, unter welchem das Reserverad und das Werkzeug placiert sind, ist mit einem dicken, filzunterlegten Vynil-Teppich ausgelegt, der sehr leicht zu reinigen ist und Gepäckstücke vor Beschädigungen wirksam schützt. Wenn die Beleuchtung eingeschaltet ist, wird beim Anheben des Deckels der Kofferraum automatisch beleuchtet.

Die im vollen Blickfeld des Fahrers liegenden Instrumente und die in bequemster Reichweite angeordneten Bedienungsschalter ersparen dem Fahrer das unangenehme Tasten und Suchen und befreien ihn von der so gefährlichen Ablenkung.

**Comfortable details and spacious usable room characterize the medium-class Jaguar.**

# NOTABLE REFINEMENTS THAT INCREASE SAFETY AND COMFORT

The interior lights are located very favorably over the middle door pillars, enhanced by additional lights in the rear of the car. The lights are turned on by opening one of the four doors. Naturally they can also be turned on by the driver independently of the door switches.

Especially large vent windows provide quick removal of stale air. The ashtrays are handily located in the armrests.

The particularly large and wide half-panorama rounded windows allow an extraordinary panoramic view.

The particularly large luggage space allows the carrying of a number of suitcases, as well as golfing equipment and small grips. The floor of the luggage space, under which the spare wheel and tools and located, is covered with a thick, felt underlaid vinyl carpet that is very easy to clean and effectively protects luggage from damage. When the lights are turned on, the luggage space is automatically lighted by raising the trunk lid

The instruments, fully within the driver's field of vision, and the easily accessible control switches spare the driver unpleasant groping and fumbling and free him from dangerous distraction.

# HIGH CLASS KOMFORT UND LUXUS

# HIGH-CLASS COMFORT AND LUXURY

Das JAGUAR-System der Innenheizung mit kombinierter Entlüftungs- und Klimatisierungs-Anlage gewährleistet eine gleichmässige Verteilung der Warmluft im ganzen Wagen. Die Warmluft wird in der gewünschten Temperatur von der Heizung in den Wagenvorderteil, und von da in Bodennähe unmittelbar in den Fond geleitet. Temperatur und Warmluftvolumen sind nach Bedarf in weitem Bereich fein regulierbar.

The JAGUAR system of interior heating and combined ventilation and air conditioning guarantees an equal apportioning of warm air to the entire car. The warm air at the desired temperature is delivered from the heater in the front of the car all the way to the back at floor level. Temperature and volume of warm air can be finely regulated over a wide range as desired.

In die Rücklehnen der Vordersitze sind millimetergenau eingepasste Klapptische eingelassen, die den Fondpassagieren mannigfache Benützungsmöglichkeiten bieten.

In the backs of the front seats are precisely fitted folding tables, which offer the rear passengers a multitude of uses.

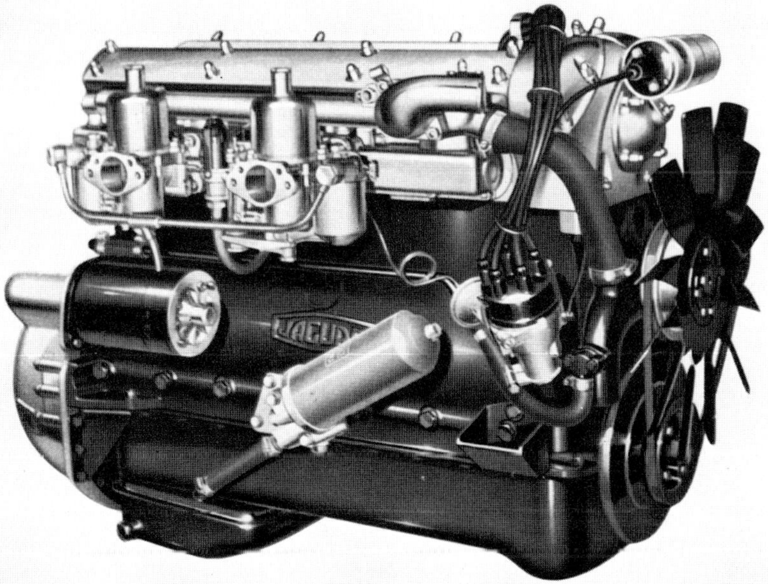

**Whoever wanted more performance could order the Mark II with the extremely high-acceleration 3.4 liter motor. But the top model was the 3.8 liter with the motor of the Mark 9 sedan, which was the top-of-the-line model made by Jaguar Cars Ltd. since 1958.**

Diese makellose "beauty" ist der 3,4 Liter XK-Motor mit den beiden obenliegenden Nockenwellen, der bei einem Hubraum von 3442 ccm und 5500 U/min 210 PS leistet. Der 3,8 Liter XK-Motor ist auf 87 mm ausgebohrt, was mit einem Hub von 106 mm einem Hubraum von 3781 ccm ergibt. Die Leistung - bei einem Verdichtungsverhältnis von 8 : 1 - erreicht 220 PS bei 5500 U/min.

This faultless "beauty" is the 3.4 liter XK motor with dual overhead camshafts, with a displacement of 3442 cc and producing 210 HP at 5500 rpm. The 3.8 liter XK motor is bored out to 87 mm, with a stroke of 106 mm, giving a displacement of 3781 cc. Its power, with a compression ratio of 8:1, is 220 HP at 5500 rpm.

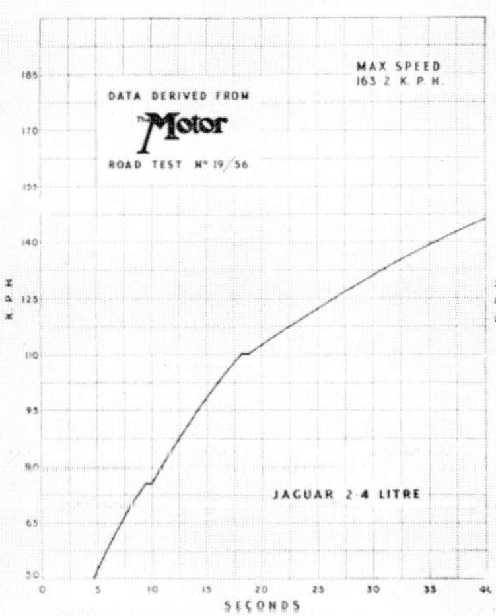


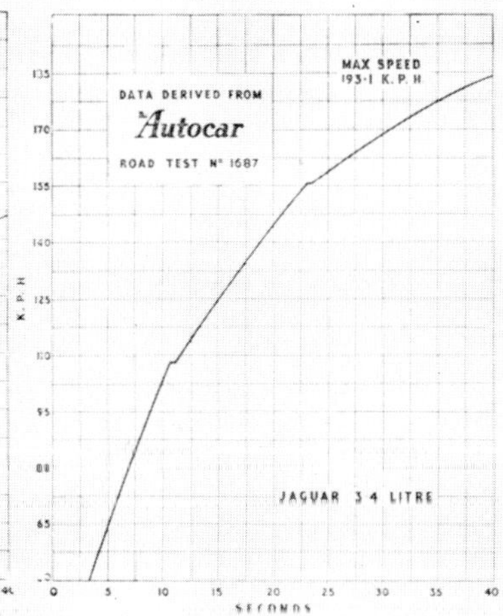


Obenstehende Messwerte über Beschleunigung und Höchstgeschwindigkeit wurden vom "MOTOR", resp. vom "AUTOCAR" in eigenen Tests ermittelt. Für den 3,8 l-Motor lagen zur Zeit der Drucklegung dieses Kataloges noch keine Messwerte von unabhängiger Seite vor.

The data above concerning acceleration and top speed were obtained in their own tests by "MOTOR" and "AUTOCAR" respectively. No independent data for the 3.8 liter motor were available when this catalog was printed.

**While the 2.4 liter motor was a short-stroke powerplant with 76.4 mm stroke compared to 83 mm bore, the 3.8 liter, with a 106 mm stroke compared to only 87 mm bore, had very different characteristics, produced tremendous torque, but withstood high engine speeds less well.**

## THE WORLD-FAMOUS XK MOTOR

The JAGUAR XK motor, as one of the most perfected, highest-performance automobile motors, enjoys high, respectful recognition all over the world, such as one would accord to a flawless crown jewel. In many challenging races, it has brought private as well as works cars to victory after victory. Along with many others, the 5 victories in the 24 Hours of Le Mans—known as the most merciless test of endurance and durability—are particularly noteworthy.
Whether it is the 2.4, 3.4 or 3.8 liter XK motor, each achieves—considering today's high standards of technology—the maximum that is attainable. Two overhead camshafts directly operate the 70-degree valves of the hemispherical combustion chambers, which are contained in specially constructed cylinder heads, protected by Weslake patents and made of a particularly suitable aluminum alloy. The massive crankshaft is carefully balanced as finely as possible. It runs in seven extraordinarily large bearings, each of 70 mm diameter, and guarantees absolutely non-flexing, non-knocking, silky-smooth running. Every stage of building and mounting these motors is dominated by implacably strict, painfully conscientious controls, ending in a four-hour test run on the test bench after assembly and a robust test drive on the road after installation in the chassis.

Probably no other motor has a better reputation for its remarkably long life and absolute reliability, even under the most difficult and oppressive conditions, than the JAGUAR XK motor.

The bore of the 2.4 liter XK motor is, at 83 mm, equal to that of the 3.4 liter motor, but the stroke is shorter, measuring only 76.5 mm. With a displacement of 2483 cc it develops 120 HP at 5750 rpm.



## DER WELTBERÜHMTE XK-MOTOR

Der JAGUAR XK-Motor geniesst als einer der vollkommensten, leistungsfähigsten Automobil-Motoren auf der ganzen Welt hohe, respektvolle Anerkennung, wie man sie einem lupenreinen Kronjuwel zollt. In zahllosen schweren und schwersten Rennen hat er sowohl private wie auch Werks-Wagen von Erfolg zu Erfolg geführt. Neben vielen anderen sind besonders die 5 Siege im 24-Stunden-Rennen von Le Mans - das als unbarmherzigste Dauer- und Zerreissprüfung bekannt ist - bemerkenswert.

Sie es nun der 2,4, der 3,4 oder der 3,8 Liter XK-Motor: jeder leistet - unter Berücksichtigung des heutigen hohen Standes der Technik - das Maximum des Erreichbaren. Zwei obenliegende Nockenwellen steuern über einen Direktantrieb die um 70° versetzten Ventile der halbkugelförmigen Verbrennungs-Kammern, die in speziell konstruierten, durch Weslake-Patente geschützten und aus einer besonders geeigneten Aluminiumlegierung gegossenen Zylinderköpfen enthalten sind. Die massive Kurbelwelle ist sorgsam und auf das Feinste ausgewuchtet. Sie läuft in sieben aussergewöhnlich grossen Lagern von je 70 mm Durchmesser und gewährleistet absolut schwingungs- und schlagfreien, seidenweichen Lauf. Jedes Fabrikations- und Montagestadium dieser Motoren wird dominiert von unerbittlich strengen, peinlich gewissenhaften Kontrollen, denen sich nach vollendetem Zusammenbau eine vierstündige Laufprobe auf dem Prüfstand und nach dem Einbau in das Chassis eine robuste Testfahrt auf der Strasse anschliessen.

Wohl kein anderer Motor besitzt einen besseren Ruf für seine unerhörte Langlebigkeit und absolute Zuverlässigkeit auch unter schwierigsten und widrigsten Betriebsbedingungen als der JAGUAR XK-Motor.

Die Bohrung des 2,4 Liter XK-Motors ist mit 83 mm gleich wie beim 3,4 Liter-Motor, aber der Hub ist kürzer; er beträgt nur 76,5 mm. Bei einem Hubvloumen von 2483 ccm entwickelt er 120 PS bei 5750 U/min.

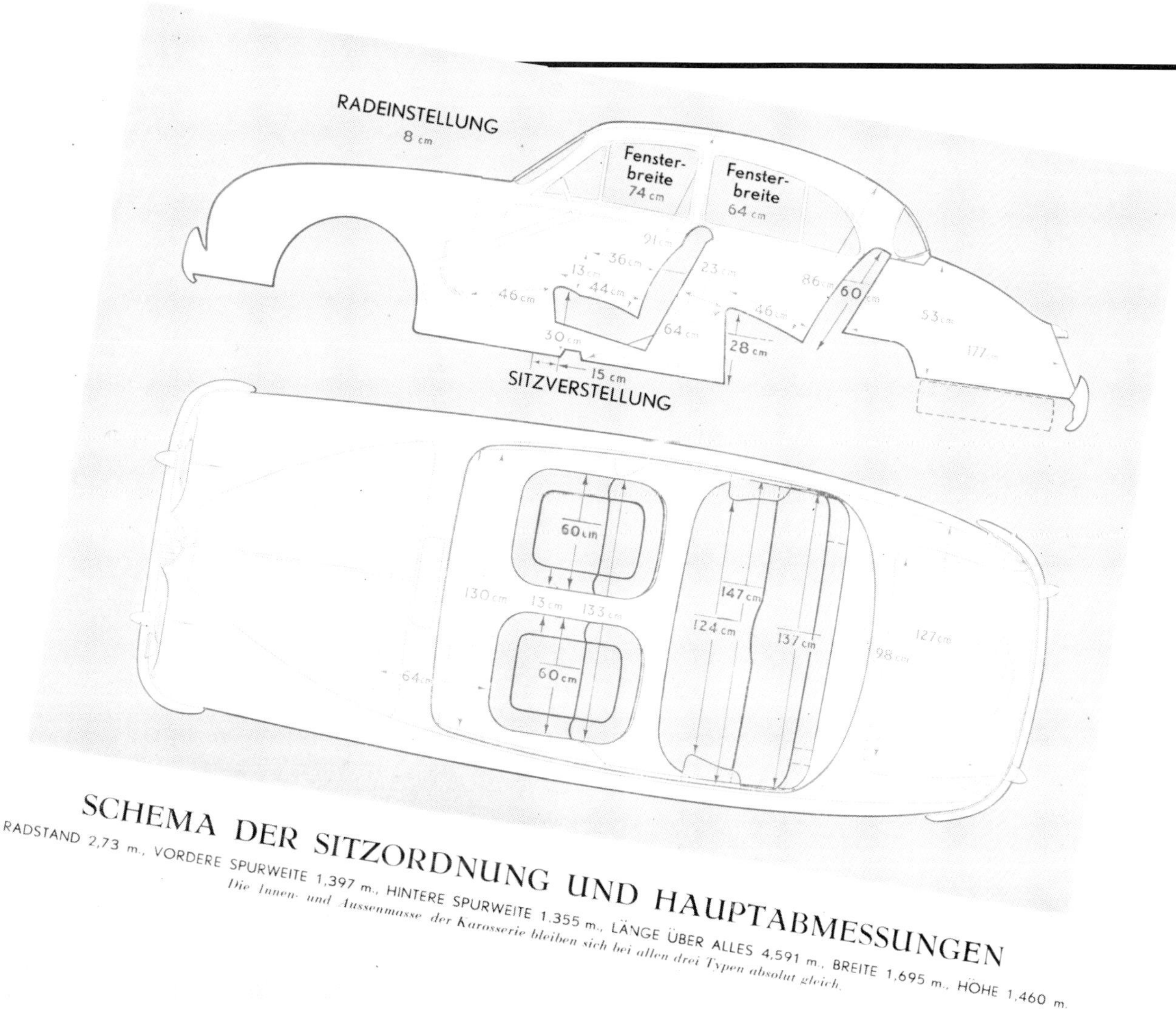


These dimensions promised comfortable sitting, in the back as well. The individual front seats were sporting in a day when bench-type seats were high in style.

## PLAN OF SEAT LOCATION AND MAIN DIMENSIONS

WHEELBASE 2.73 m, FRONT TRACK 1.397 m, REAR TRACK 1355 m, OVERALL LENGTH 4591 m, WIDTH 1695 m, HEIGHT 1460 m.

The inner and outer dimensions of the body are absolutely identical for all three types.

F A R B E N T A F E L

Die nachstehend aufgeführten Farbkombinationen entsprechen der Standard-Ausführung. Jede Abweichung, die eine Sonderbehandlung der Karosserie und/oder der Polster notwendig macht, bedingt einen Aufpreis, der bei Bestellungsannahme bekannt gegeben wird.

| KAROSSERIE | POLSTER |
|---|---|
| pearl gray | red, light blue, dark blue, gray |
| chestnut brown | chestnut brown |
| cream | red, light blue, dark blue |
| burgundy | red, chestnut brown |
| Cotswald | blue, dark blue, gray |
| black | red, tan, gray |
| mist gray | red, light blue, dark blue, gray |
| Sherwood green | tan, Swedish green |
| British racing green | tan, Swedish green |
| Cornish gray | red, light blue, dark blue, gray |

Abbildungen unverbindlich. Änderungen vorbehalten.

## COLOR CHART

The following color combinations represent standard production. Any change that necessitates special treatment of the body and/or the upholstery requires an additional price, which will be stated when the order is taken.

| BODY | UPHOLSTERY |
|---|---|
| pearl gray | red, light blue, dark blue, gray |
| chestnut brown | chestnut brown |
| cream | red, light blue, dark blue |
| burgundy | red, chestnut brown |
| Cotswold | blue dark blue, gray |
| black | red, tan, gray |
| mist gray | red, light blue, dark blue, gray |
| Sherwood | green tan, Swedish green |
| British racing green | tan, Swedish green |
| Cornish gray | red, light blue, dark blue, gray |

Illustrations not binding, variation rights reserved.

**The 3.8 Liter, top model of the Mark II series, had four disc brakes as standard equipment and could be ordered with Borg-Warner automatic transmission. A large number of the cars so prepared were sold in the USA, which became a more and more important sales market for Jaguar.**

# The New Jaguar 3.8

Polished walnut instrument panel; housing for radio, speaker, heater controls and ashtray.

Walnut flush-fitting occasional tables; soft leather upholstery over foam rubber.

Ample luggage compartment—13½ cubic feet capacity, with automatic interior light.

## OUTSTANDING FEATURES OF THE 3.8 SEDAN

- Power assisted steering, as an optional extra.
- 3.8 Litre engine.
- Entirely new dashboard layout. It includes revolution counter and speedometer directly in front of the driver, and separate instruments for oil pressure, water temperature, fuel gauge and ammeter.
- Dunlop disc brakes, featuring quick change pads.
- Large windshield with very slim pillars and wrap-around rear window.
- Front seats adjustable for height as well as reach.
- Automatic transmission, featuring a finger-tip control by which intermediate gear may be held indefinitely, or four-speed and reverse manual shift with overdrive.
- New high output heating and defrosting system, with separate duct to rear compartment, operated by two-speed fan, controlled by switch on instrument panel.
- Flush fitting occasional tables in rear compartment.
- Two-spoke adjustable steering wheel with semi-circular horn ring.
- Separate housing below instrument panel containing a radio and speaker, optional extra, together with heater controls and a very large ash tray.

**Though the 3.8 Liter reached almost 200 kph, the 3.4 liter was not exactly underpowered. The lack of 10 HP was scarcely noticeable when driving; the 3.4 Liter was one of the fastest family sedans in Europe during the early Sixties.**

# 3·4 LITRE SPECIFICATION

THE JAGUAR "B" TYPE ENGINE

This is the world famous double overhead camshaft engine specially developed for the 3.4 litre. Most of the special features once only supplied on modified XK engines are now incorporated in the "B" type engine as standard equipment. High lift cams, special head, double exhaust system and the new twin S.U. H.D.6 carburettors are regular equipment and the power developed is 210 b.h.p. at 5,500 r.p.m. The camshaft and chain case covers are brilliantly polished, the exhaust manifolds are finished in smooth, gleaming black enamel. Built to the highest precision standards, every Jaguar engine is individually bench tested for over four hours.

**ENGINE.** Special 6-cylinder 3.4-litre "blue-top" engine with "B" type head. High lift cams. Twin S.U. type H.D.6 carburettors and double exhaust system. Develops 210 b.h.p. at 5,500 r.p.m. 70° twin overhead camshafts driven by two-stage roller chain. 83 mm. bore x 106 mm. stroke. Cubic capacity 3,442 c.c. (210 cu. ins.). Compression ratio 8 to 1 (7 to 1 optional). Cooling by pump and fan with by-pass thermostat control. Forced lubrication by submerged pump system incorporating full-flow filter. Chrome iron cylinder block. Cylinder head of high tensile aluminium alloy with hemispherical combustion chambers. Aluminium alloy pistons. Steel connecting rods. 2¾" diameter counterweighted crankshaft carried in seven large steel-backed bearings.

**TRANSMISSION (manually operated gearbox).** Four-speed single helical synchromesh gearbox. Centrally positioned gear-shift lever. Gear ratios: 1st and reverse, 10.55; 2nd, 6.20; 3rd, 4.28; 4th, 3.54. Borg & Beck 10" single dry-plate clutch with hydraulic operation. Hardy-Spicer propeller shaft. Hypoid rear axle.

**TRANSMISSION (Automatic Transmission Model).** Borg-Warner Automatic Transmission system giving following ratios: Direct, 3.54; intermediate, 5.3 to 10.95; low, 8.16 to 17.6. Hardy-Spicer propeller shaft. Hypoid rear axle.

**TRANSMISSION (Overdrive Model).** Gear ratios: 1st and reverse, 11.23; 2nd, 6.6; 3rd, 4.56; Top, 3.77; Overdrive 2.93.

**SUSPENSION.** Independent front suspension incorporating semi-trailing wishbones and coil springs with telescopic shock absorbers. Trailing link rear suspension by cantilever semi-elliptic leaf springs, radius arms and telescopic shock absorbers.

**BRAKES.** Lockheed "Brakemaster" servo-assisted self-adjusting hydraulic brakes. Brake drum diameter 11⅛". Friction lining area 157 sq. ins. "Pull-up" handbrake lever mounted at floor level.

**STEERING.** Burman re-circulating ball-type steering with 17" diameter adjustable steering wheel. 3½ turns from lock to lock. Turning circle 33½ ft.

**WHEELS AND TYRES.** Pressed steel bolt-on disc wheels fitted with Dunlop 6.40 x 15 in. "ROADSPEED" tyres. Spare wheel and tyre.

**FUEL SUPPLY.** Twelve Imperial gallons tank capacity. S.U. electric pump.

**ELECTRICAL EQUIPMENT AND INSTRUMENTS.** Lucas 12 volt battery. 51 amp. hour at 10 hour rate with current voltage control. Ventilated dynamo. Side lamps, headlamps with dipper control, integral stop tail lamps with built-in reflectors, reversing lamps, self-cancelling flashing direction indicators with warning light, instrument panel lights, courtesy lights, twin-blended note horns, twin-blade two-speed, self-parking, wind-shield wipers, 5" diameter speedometer, 5" diameter revolution counter, ammeter, oil pressure gauge, water temperature gauge, fuel gauge with warning light.

**BODY.** All steel full 5-seater saloon. Integral body chassis construction. Four doors. Seats upholstered in finest quality leather over deep foam rubber. Front bucket seats (except on Automatic Transmission model which has bench-type seat). Polished walnut instrument panel and interior garnishings. Two glove compartments. Ashtrays. Armrests to all doors and central folding armrest in rear. Interior sun visors. Deep pile carpets over thick felt underlay. Heavy duty bumpers with overriders front and rear.

**LUGGAGE ACCOMMODATION.** Ample luggage accommodation is provided in a capacious rear locker fitted with an automatic light. 13½ cubic feet of luggage space available.

**SPARE WHEEL AND TOOLS.** The spare wheel is carried beneath the boot floor in a separate compartment and is readily accessible. Kit of tools, jack and wheelbrace.

**JACKING.** Exterior jacking posts front and rear, enable the car to be lifted with the minimum of effort by means of the jack provided.

**PRINCIPAL DIMENSIONS.** Wheelbase, 8 ft. 11⅜ ins.; track front, 4 ft. 6⅝ ins.; track rear, 4 ft. 2⅛ ins.; overall length, 15 ft. 0¾ ins.; overall width, 5 ft. 6¾ ins.; overall height, 4 ft. 9½ ins.; ground clearance, 7 ins.; turning circle, 33 ft. 6 ins.; dry weight, 27 cwt. approx.

A THOROUGHBRED IN THE TRUE JAGUAR TRADITION

The 3.4 and 3.8 liter versions of the Mark II combined, along with really impressive styling, the characteristics of comfortable touring sedans and the sporting performance of high—caliber sports cars. a type of transport that even today has none of its timeliness.

## SEDAN LUXURY - - - SUPER SPORTS CAR PERFORMANCE

*Here is passenger comfort of the highest order. Soft tanned leather upholstery over Dunlopillo foam rubber. Side armrests to all doors and centrally positioned folding armrest in rear compartment. Beautifully figured hand rubbed walnut cabinet work. Deep pile carpets. Ventilating windows. Interior lighting. Ashtrays.*

HERE is the perfect car for the motorist whose needs preclude ownership of the open or coupe type of sports car yet who demands all the exhilaration of true sports car performance. With the renowned Jaguar XK double overhead camshaft engine, exactly as fitted to the famous Jaguar sports models, dynamic acceleration is linked with a top speed maximum of over 120 m.p.h.

Built for the driver who understands and demands sports car characteristics, the stability, cornering and general roadholding qualities measure up to the most critical requirements, whilst steering and braking are such that inspire immediate confidence. Truly the car for the sports car enthusiast who need sacrifice nothing in order to enjoy the satisfaction that sports car ownership brings. Passenger accommodation is unrestricted—five people can be carried in comfort. Luggage accommodation is equally generous, for 13½ cubic feet capacity is available. Whatever the climate may be, complete sedan comfort and protection are afforded. Finally, an entirely new experience awaits the owner of a 3.4 litre Jaguar—a degree of silence that is extraordinary in any kind of car and almost unbelievable in a car giving sports car performance. Not a trace of engine noise reaches the interior, no road noises are transmitted, and wind rush is reduced to no more than a whisper at even the highest speeds.

Here, then, is the car built to the specification that thousands of sports car enthusiasts have so long demanded. Super sports car performance, full passenger and luggage accommodation, compact overall dimensions, complete weather protection. All this and a Jaguar, too!

**SEE WHAT THE** *Three-point-four* **GIVES YOU**

**✶ The world famous Le Mans bred Jaguar XK engine ✶ Over 120 m.p.h. maximum speed ✶ Amazing acceleration, 0—60 m.p.h. in 11 seconds ✶ Seating for five people ✶ Finest real leather upholstery ✶ 13½ cubic feet luggage capacity ✶ Compact dimensions for easy parking ✶ Automatic Transmission, Overdrive or Manual Gearshift to choice**

## A THOROUGHBRED IN THE TRUE JAGUAR TRADITION

Pictures like these make sales literature from the Jaguar firm desirable collectors'items too. The spoked wheels shown in this picture could be had for a slight extra charge and especially stressed the thoroughbred character of the car.

**In its basic form, the Mark II was delivered with these disc wheels, which symbolize elegance, particularly along with the whitewall tires that were then highly fashionable. Right: a pleasure to sit behind such a splendid hardwood dashboard, calmly operate the many control switches, and keep an eye on the classically beautiful and easily readable Smiths intruments, while the gauges hurried upward...**

# MONY OF PRACTICAL BILITY AND REFINED UTY

# HARMONIE ZWECKMÄSSIGER UEBERSICHTLICHKEIT UND GEDIEGENER SCHÖNHEIT

Names of the instruments and control switches

1. Ammeter.
2. Fuel gauge.
3. Outside light switch.
4. Oil pressure gauge.
5. Water thermometer.
6. Speedometer with odometer.
7. Electric clock.
8. Tachometer.
9. Choke (only in 2.4 Liter model).
0. Overdrive switch.
1. Interior light switch.
2. Dashboard light switch.
3. Heater vent.
4. Ignition lock.
5. Cigarette lighter.
6. Starter button.
7. Map reading light.
8. Electric windshield wiper switch.
9. Electric windshield washer switch.
20. Directional light lever.
21. Clock-setting control.
22. High-beam indicator.
23. Horn ring.
24. Automatic transmission control.
25. Daily odometer control.
26. Automatic transmission lever.
27. Heater duct control.
28. Heater temperature control.
29. Radio control.
30. Radio control.
31. Smoke-free ashtray.
32. Ventilator control.
33. Brake fluid gauge.

## Bezeichnung der Instrumente und Bedienungsschalter

1. *Ampèremeter.*
2. *Benzinstandsanzeiger.*
3. *Schalter für Aussenlichter.*
4. *Oeldruckmesser.*
5. *Kuhlwasser-Thermometer.*
6. *Geschwindigkeitsmesser mit Totalisator.*
7. *Elektrische Uhr.*
8. *Tourenzähler.*
9. *Choke (nur beim 2.4 Liter-Modell).*
10. *Schalter für Overdrive.*
11. *Innenbeleuchtung.*
12. *Instrumenten-Beleuchtung.*
13. *Heizungsventilator.*
14. *Zündschloss*
15. *Zigarettenanzünder.*
16. *Starterknopf.*
17. *Kartenbeleuchtung.*
18. *Elektrische Scheibenwischer.*
19. *Elektrische Scheibenwaschanlage.*
20. *Blinkschalter.*
21. *Uhreinstellung.*
22. *Abblendschalter.*
23. *Signalring.*
24. *Schaltschema fur automatisches Getriebe.*
25. *Wegstreckenmesser Einstellung.*
26. *Schalthebеn für automatisches Getriebe.*
27. *Heizung (Strömungsregler).*
28. *Heizung (Temperaturregler).*
29. *Radiobedienung.*
30. *Radiobedienung.*
31. *Rauchfreier Aschenbecher.*
32. *Bedienung der Entlüftungsklappe.*
33. *Bremsflüssigkeitsstandsanzeiger.*

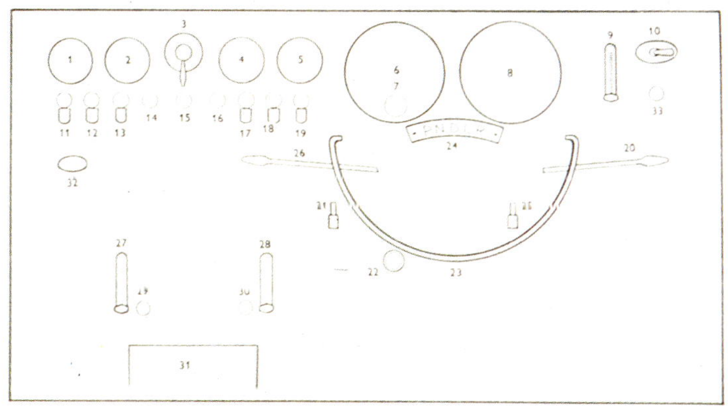

Clearly visible in direct contrast are the effective body changes in the Mark II. In its forerunner one could get disc brakes only as special equipment. A relic of olden days is the large antique-style four-spoke steering wheel in the so-called Mark I.

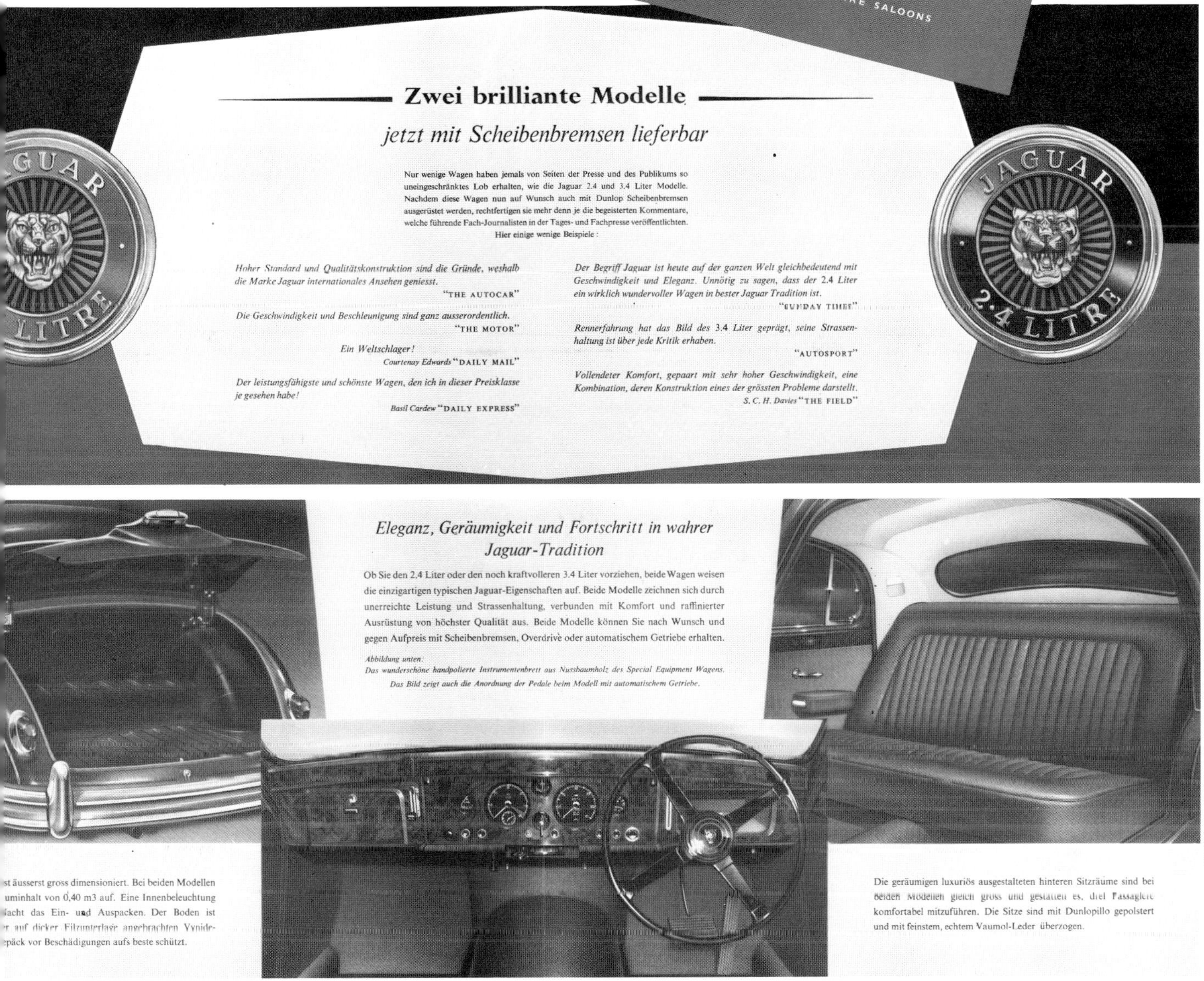

## Zwei brilliante Modelle

*jetzt mit Scheibenbremsen lieferbar*

Nur wenige Wagen haben jemals von Seiten der Presse und des Publikums so uneingeschränktes Lob erhalten, wie die Jaguar 2.4 und 3.4 Liter Modelle. Nachdem diese Wagen nun auf Wunsch auch mit Dunlop Scheibenbremsen ausgerüstet werden, rechtfertigen sie mehr denn je die begeisterten Kommentare, welche führende Fach-Journalisten in der Tages- und Fachpresse veröffentlichten.
Hier einige wenige Beispiele:

*Hoher Standard und Qualitätskonstruktion sind die Gründe, weshalb die Marke Jaguar internationales Ansehen geniesst.*
"THE AUTOCAR"

*Die Geschwindigkeit und Beschleunigung sind ganz ausserordentlich.*
"THE MOTOR"

*Ein Weltschlager!*
*Courtenay Edwards* "DAILY MAIL"

*Der leistungsfähigste und schönste Wagen, den ich in dieser Preisklasse je gesehen habe!*
*Basil Cardew* "DAILY EXPRESS"

*Der Begriff Jaguar ist heute auf der ganzen Welt gleichbedeutend mit Geschwindigkeit und Eleganz. Unnötig zu sagen, dass der 2.4 Liter ein wirklich wundervoller Wagen in bester Jaguar Tradition ist.*
"SUNDAY TIMES"

*Rennerfahrung hat das Bild des 3.4 Liter geprägt, seine Strassenhaltung ist über jede Kritik erhaben.*
"AUTOSPORT"

*Vollendeter Komfort, gepaart mit sehr hoher Geschwindigkeit, eine Kombination, deren Konstruktion eines der grössten Probleme darstellt.*
*S. C. H. Davies* "THE FIELD"

*Eleganz, Geräumigkeit und Fortschritt in wahrer Jaguar-Tradition*

Ob Sie den 2.4 Liter oder den noch kraftvolleren 3.4 Liter vorziehen, beide Wagen weisen die einzigartigen typischen Jaguar-Eigenschaften auf. Beide Modelle zeichnen sich durch unerreichte Leistung und Strassenhaltung, verbunden mit Komfort und raffinierter Ausrüstung von höchster Qualität aus. Beide Modelle können Sie nach Wunsch und gegen Aufpreis mit Scheibenbremsen, Overdrive oder automatischem Getriebe erhalten.

*Abbildung unten:*
*Das wunderschöne handpolierte Instrumentenbrett aus Nussbaumholz des Special Equipment Wagens. Das Bild zeigt auch die Anordnung der Pedale beim Modell mit automatischem Getriebe.*

...st äusserst gross dimensioniert. Bei beiden Modellen ...uminhalt von 0,40 m3 auf. Eine Innenbeleuchtung ...lacht das Ein- und Auspacken. Der Boden ist ...r auf dicker Filzunterlage angebrachten Vynide-...päck vor Beschädigungen aufs beste schützt.

Die geräumigen luxuriös ausgestalteten hinteren Sitzräume sind bei beiden Modellen gleich gross und gestatten es, drei Passagiere komfortabel mitzuführen. Die Sitze sind mit Dunlopillo gepolstert und mit feinstem, echtem Vaumol-Leder überzogen.

## Two Brilliant Models

### Now Available with Disc Brakes

Very few models have received such unlimited praise from the press and the public as the Jaguar 2.4 and 3.4 liter models. After these cars were optionally fitted with Dunlop disc brakes, they justified all the more the enthusiastic comments that leading specialist journalists published in the daily and specialist press. Here are a few examples:

High standards and quality construction are the reasons why the Jaguar marque enjoys international renown.

"THE AUTOCAR"

The speed and acceleration are quite extraordinary.

"THE MOTOR"

A world—leaper.

Courtney Edwards, "DAILY EXPRESS"

The Jaguar concept is synonymous with speed and elegance all over the world today. Needless to say that the 2.4 Liter is a really wonderful car in the best Jaguar tradition.

"SUNDAY TIMES"

Racing experience has characterized the nature of the 3.4 Liter; its roadholding is above all criticism.

"AUTOSPORT"

Complete comfort, along with very high speed, a combination whose construction presents one of the greatest problems.

S.C.H. Davis, "THE FIELD"

Elegance, Roominess and Progress in the true Jaguar tradition.
Whether you prefer the 2.4 Liter or the even more powerful 3.4 Liter, both cars show the unique, typical Jaguar characteristics. Both models stand out through their unequaled performance and roadhandling, along with comfort and refined highest—quality equipment. You can obtain both models optionally, at a higher price, with disc brakes, overdrive or automatic transmission.
The luggage space is extremely large. In both models it has a volume of 0.40 cubic meters. Interior lighting makes loading and unloading at night easier. The floor is covered with a Vynide carpet on a thick felt underlay, that best protects your luggage from damage.
The roomy, luxuriously appointed rear seat area is equally large in both models and allows three passengers to ride comfortably. The seats are upholstered with Dunlopillo and covered with the finest genuine Vaumol leather.

Naturally one could obtain such a fascinating automobile in a great number of tasteful color combinations, whereby the choice was not exactly made easy for Anglophiles with names like "Cotswold Blue" and "Sherwood Green".

F A R B E N T A F E L

Die nachstehend aufgeführten Farbkombinationen entsprechen der Standard-Ausführung. Jede Abweichung, die eine Sonderbehandlung der Karosserie und/oder der Polster notwendig macht, bedingt einen Aufpreis, der bei Bestellungsannahme bekannt gegeben wird.

| KAROSSERIE | INNENAUSSTATTUNG |
|---|---|
| Cream | Red, Light Blue, Dark Blue |
| Pearl Grey | Red, Light Blue, Dark Blue, Grey, Maroon |
| Mist Grey | Red, Light Blue, Dark Blue, Grey, Maroon |
| Cotswold Blue | Light Blue, Dark Blue, Grey |
| Sherwood Green | Tan, Light Tan, Suede Green |
| Black | Red, Grey, Tan, Light Tan |
| Carmen Red | Red |
| Opalescent Gunmetal Grey | Red, Light Blue, Dark Blue, Beige, Grey, Maroon |
| Opalescent Silver Grey | Red, Light Blue, Dark Blue, Grey, Maroon |
| Opalescent Silver Blue | Dark Blue, Grey |
| Opalescent Blue | Light Blue, Grey, Red |
| Golden Sand | Light Tan, Red |
| Opalescent Dark Green | Suede Green, Tan, Light Tan |
| Opalescent Maroon | Maroon, Beige |

ABBILDUNGEN UNVERBINDLICH. ÄNDERUNGEN VORBEHALTEN.

## COLOR CHART

The color combinations listed here represent standard production. Any deviation that necessitates special treatment of the body and/or the upholstery requires an extra price which will be stated when ordering.

BODY INTERIOR

Descriptions not binding, right to make changes reserved.

**Under the hood one recognized the stronger 3.4 Liter version at once by the blue-painted cylinder head covers. The special equipment was only for the 2.4; features such as are listed at bottom right were standard in the 3.4 and 3.8 Liter versions.**

## THE 3.4 LITRE

**MOTOR:** Special 6-cylinder 3.4 liter "blue top" XK motor with B-type cylinder head. High valve form. Dual SU carburetor (Type H.D. 6) and dual exhaust system. Bore 83 mm, stroke 106 mm. Displacement 3.442 liters. Compression ratio 8:1 (7:1 optionally). Produces 213 HP at 5500 rpm. Overhead camshafts with two-stage roller chain drive, valves inclined at 70 degrees. Water cooling regulated by thermostat and by-pass, with pump and fan. Pressure lubrication by oil pump located in sump and built-in mainstream oil filter. Cylinder block of chrome-alloy cast iron. Cylinder head of aluminum alloy with high rigidity. Hemispherical combustion chambers . Pistons of aluminum alloy. Steel connecting rods. Balanced crankshaft with 7 bearings, large trunnions of 70 mm diameter.

**TRANSMISSION (Standard drive):** 4-speed synchronized gearbox, diagonally geared. Gearshift lever mounted centrally between the two front seats. Gear ratios: First and reverse gears: 11.95:1, second gear: 7.10:1, third gear: 4.84:1, fourth gear: 3.54:1. Hydraulically activated 10-inch Borg & Beck single-plate clutch. Hardy Spicer universal joint. Hypoid differential.

**TRANSMISSION (Model with fast gear):** Same gears as above, but with built in Laycock-de Normanville fast gear which is activated by a switch on the dashboard. Gear ratios: First and reverse gears: 11.33:1, second gear: 6.60:1, third gear: 4.56:1, direct gear: 3.77:1, fast gear: 2.93:1.

**TRANSMISSION (Automatic transmission):** Automatic Borg-Warner transmission system with possibility of blocking the middle gear. Gear ratios: small gear: 17.6 to 8.16:1, middle gear: 10.95 to 5.08:1, direct gear: 3.54:1.

**SUSPENSION:** Independent front suspension with wishbone transverse links and hydraulic shock absorbers. Rear suspension on long semi-elliptic leaf springs and longitudinal links, with hydraulic shock absorbers.

**BRAKES:** Self-adjusting hydraulic Lockheed "Brake-Master" brakes with servo assistance. Brake drum diameer 282 mm. Total braking surface 1013 square cm. (Optionally, Dunlop disc brakes on all four wheels.) "Pull-up" hand brake, lever mounted on floor.

**STEERING:** "Burman" ball-joint steering with adjustable steering wheel of 432 mm diameter. 3.5 revolutions from block to block. Turning circle 10.2 meters.

**WHEELS AND TIRES:** Pressed steel disc wheels with lug bolts. Dunlop Road Speed tires (6.40 x 15). Spoked wheels available optionally for vehicles with disc brakes. Spare wheel.

**FUEL SYSTEM:** Electric SU fuel pump. Tank capacity 54 liters.

**ELECTRICAL EQUIPMENT AND INSTRUMENTS:** 12-volt Lucas battery (capacity 51 amp./std./10h) with combined current/tension regulator. Air-cooled generator. Separate built-in side lights and headlights with high and low beams. Dual fog lights. Combined brake and taillights, plus back-up light. Automatically shutting-off directional signals with warning signal. Interior lighting, two cigarette lighters. Tuned double horn. Two windshield wipers with 2 speeds and automatic return. Electric starter. Distributor head with automatic vacuum and centrally controlled ignition distribution. Oil-bath coil. Large tachometer and speedometer of 127 mm diameter. Electric clock. Ammeter, oil pressure gauge, water thermometer and fuel gauge with warning light.

**BODYWORK:** 5-seat self-supporting all-steel body, providing maximum rigidity with minimum weight. Four doors. Foam rubber upholstery covered with finest leather. Adjustable separate front seats (Models with automatic transmission have a complete front seat bench). Polished walnut instrument panel and inner decoration. Two glove compartments, one of them locking. Ash tray. Two sun visors. Armrests on all doors, plus folding armrests in the middle of the rear seat. Moquette carpets over thick felt underlays. Heating and defrosting system. Windshield washer system. Strong wraparound bumpers with overiders.

**LUGGAGE COMPARTMENT:** Roomy locking trunk of 4 square dm capacity with automatic interior light.

**SPARE WHEEL AND TOOLS:** Spare wheel easily accessible in a seperate compartment under the luggage compartment floor. The tools are in a special case which is located in the same compartment as the spare tire, along with the auto jack and lug wrench. (Models with spoked wheels also have a special hammer.)

**JACKING THE CAR:** Front and rear attachment points on both sides of the body allow easy application of the jack and lifting of the car with minimal strength.

**MAIN DIMENSIONS:** Wheelbase: 2.73 meters, front track: 1.39 meters, rear track: 1.27 meters, overall length: 4.59 meters, overall width: 1.70 meters, overall height: 1.46 meters, ground clearance: 0.18 meter, turning circle: 10.2 meters, dry weight. approx. 1970 kg.

## THE 2.4 LITRE

**MOTOR:** Six-cylinder 2.4 liter XK motor. Overhead camshafts with two-stage roller-chain drive. Valve angle 70 degrees. Bore 83 mm, stroke 76.5 mm, displacement 2.483 liters. Produces 114 HP at 5750 rpm. Compression ratio 8:1 (optionally 7:1). Dual Solex downdraft carburetor. Water cooling regulated by thermostat and by-pass, with pump and fan. Pressure lubrication by oil pump located in sump and built-in mainstream oil filter. Cylinder block of chrome-alloy cast iron. Cylinder head of aluminum alloy with high rigidity. Hemispherical combustion chambers. Pistons of aluminum alloy. Steel connecting rods. Balanced crankshaft with 7 bearings and large trunnions of 70 mm diameter.

**TRANSMISSION (Standard drive):** 4-speed synchromesh gearbox, diagonally geared. Gearshift lever mounted centrally between the two front seats. Gear ratios: First and reverse gears: 14.41:1, second gear: 8.46:1, third gear: 5.84:1, fourth gear: 4.27:1. Hydraulically activated 9-inch Borg & Beck single-plate clutch. Hardy Spicer universal joint. Hypoid differential.

**TRANSMISSION (Model with fast gear):** Same gears as above, but with built-in Laycock-de Normanville fast gear activated by a switch on the dashboard. Gear ratios: first and reverse gears: 13.56:1, second gear: 7.96:1, third gear: 5.5):1, direct gear: 4.55:1, fast gear: 3.54:1.

**TRANSMISSION (Automatic transmission):** Automatic Borg-Warner transmission system with possibility of blocking middle gear. Gear ratios: small gear: 21.2 to 9.86:1, middle gear 13.20 to 6.14:1, direct gear: 4.27:1.

**SUSPENSION:** Independent front suspension with wishbone transverse links and hydraulic shock absorbers. Rear suspension with long semi-elliptic leaf springs and longitudinal links, plus hydraulic shock absorbers.

**BRAKES:** Self-adjusting hydraulic Lockheed "Brake-Master" brakes with servo assistance. Brake drum diameter 282 mm. Total braking surface 1013 square cm. (Optionally, Dunlop disc brakes on all 4 wheels). "Pull-up" hand brake lever mounted on floor.

**STEERING:** "Burman" ball-joint steering with adjustable steering wheel of 432 mm diameter. 3.5 revolutions from block to block. Turning circle 10.2 meters.

**WHEELS AND TIRES:** Pressed steel disc wheels with lug bolts. Dunlop Super Balloon tires (6.40 x 15). Spoked wheels optionally available for cars with disc brakes. Spare wheel.

**FUEL SYSTEM:** Electric SU fuel pump. Tank capacity 54 liters.

**ELECTRICAL EQUIPMENT AND INSTRUMENTS:** 12-voly Lucas battery (capacity 51 amp./std./10h) with combined current/tension regulator. Air-cooled generator. Separate built-in side lights and headlights with high and low beams. Combined brake and taillights plus back-up light. Automatically turning-off directional lights with warning signal. Tuned double horn. Dual windshield wipers with two speeds and automatic return. Electric starter. Distributor head with automatic vacuum and centrally controlled distribution. Oil-bath coil. Large speedometer of 127 mm diameter. Ammeter, oil-pressure gauge, water thermometer and fuel gauge with warning light.

**BODYWORK:** Five-seat self-supporting all-steel body, providing maximum rigidity with minimum weight. Four doors. Foam rubber upholstery covered with finest leather. Adjustable separate front seats. (Models with automatic transmission have complete aeat bench). Polished walnut instrument panel and interior decoration. Two glove compartments, one of them locking. Ash tray. Two sun visors. Moquette carpets over thick felt underlays. Strong wrap-around bumpers with overriders.

**LUGGAGE SPACE:** Roomy locking trunk of 4 cubic dm capacity with sutomatic interior light.

**SPARE WHEEL AND TOOLS:** Spare wheel easily accessible in a separate compartment under the luggage space. The tools are kept in a special case which is located in the same compartment with the spare wheel, along with the auto jack and lug wrench (Models with spoked wheels also have a special hammer).

**JACKING THE CAR:** Front and rear attachment points on both sides of the body allow easy application of the jack and lifting the car with minimal energy.

**MAIN DIMENSIONS:** Wheelbase: 2.73 meters, front track: 1.39 meters, rear track: 1.27 meters, overall length: 4.59 meters, overall width: 1.70 meters, overall height: 1.46 meters, ground clearance: 0.18 meter, turning circle 10.2 meters, dry weight approx. 1320 kg.

**MODEL WITH SPECIAL EQUIPMENT:** The 2.4 Liter "Special Equipment" is delivered with heating and defroster system, folding armrest in the middle of the back seat, windshield washer system, dual fog lights, interior light activated by the doors, tachometer with electric clock, cigarette lighter, enameled exhaust pipe.

**Pictures from a small sales catalog with the entire Jaguar program including the legendary E-Type.**

# JAGUAR
## MK 2

Sport sedan, with choice of 2.4, 3.4 or 3.8 liter motor

**MOTOR:** Six-cylinder XK motor with dual overhead camshafts at 70 degrees, two carburetors, compression ratio 8:1.
**2.4 Liter:** Bore 83 mm x stroke 76.5 mm, displacement 2483 cc, 120 HP at 5750 rpm, 19.8 mkg at 2000 rpm.
**3.4 Liter:** Bore 83 mm x stroke 106 mm, displacement 3442 cc, 210 HP at 5500 rpm, 29.7 mkg at 3000 rpm.
**3.8 Liter:** Bore 87 mm x stroke 106 mm, displacement 3781 cc, 220 HP at 5500 rpm, 33.1 mkg at 3000 rpm.

**GEARS:** Fully synchronized 4-speed gearbox, stick shift. A fast gear (overdrive) can be switched onto fourth gear by means of a switch on the steering column.
Optional fully automatic transmission (Hydraulic torque converter and 3-speed planetary gears). Selector lever on steering column.

**SUSPENSION:** Front wishbone transverse links, coil springs, telescopic shock absorbers and torsion stabilizer. Rigid rear axle with quarter-elliptic leaf springs, longitudinal links, telescopic shock absorbers and Panhard bar. The 3.8 Liter model has a standard limited-slip differential.

**BRAKES:** Four-wheel disc brakes with servo assistance, self-adjusting. Hand brake, self-adjusting, works mechanically on the rear wheels.

**STEERING:** Ball-joint steering. Adjustable steering column.

**WHEELS AND TIRES:** 6.40x15 (185x15) with tubes. Spoked wheels with central hubcaps optional.

**FUEL SYSTEM:** Electric fuel pump, 55-liter tank capacity.

**ELECTRIC EQUIPMENT AND INSTRUMENTS:** 12-volt system. Fog lights, back-up light, two-speed windshield wipers, windshield washing system, flashers, tachometer, ammeter, clock, cigarette lighter etc.

**BODYWORK:** Self-supporting safety body, 4 doors, 5 seats, leather upholstery, velour carpets, folding rear armrest; instrument panel of polished fine-veined walnut wood; trunk capacity 400 liters; spare wheel and tools under the luggage space floor.

**HEATING AND VENTILATION:** Fresh-air heating system for front and rear, with two-speed fan.

**MAIN DIMENSIONS:** Wheelbase 273 cm, front track 141 cm, rear track 137 cm, length 459 cm, width 170 cm, height 143 cm, turning circle 10.2 meters.

# 420/420G: Alternatives at Low Prices . . .

In the fall of 1966 the exclusive Jaguar Mark X gave rise to the Type 420, which, as its designation indicates, had a 4.2-liter motor and, with its inward-tilted grille, stylistically anticipated the XJ. The 420 had about 10 HP less than the G-model, which was available until 1970 (the 420 until 1968). These cars could also be had in a Daimler version—as the Sovereign model. With a top speed of almost 200 kph, the 420 was one of the fastest sedans of its time, and also embodied the understated elegance that was always typical of Jaguar. Fewer than 20,000 of these two variations were made.

# JAGUAR

420

Schnelle, repräsentative Reise-Limousine

**MOTOR**: Sechszylinder „XK"-Motor mit zwei obenliegenden Nockenwellen und zwei Vergasern. Verdichtung 8 : 1, Bohrung 92,07 mm × Hub 106 mm. Zylinderinhalt 4235 ccm; 245 PS bei 5500 U/min; 39 mkg bei 4000 U/min. Ventilatorsteuerung über temperaturabhängige Viskosekupplung.

**GETRIEBE**: Vollsynchronisiertes 4-Gang-Getriebe, Knüppelschaltung. Ein Schnellgang (Overdrive) kann durch einen Schalter an der Lenksäule zum vierten Gang zugeschaltet werden.
Gegen Aufpreis vollautomatisches Getriebe (Hydr. Drehmomentwandler und 3-Gang-Planetengetriebe) mit zwei Fahrbereichen (D 1 / D 2), von denen einer wahlweise auch geschaltet werden kann.

**RADAUFHÄNGUNG**: Vorn Trapez-Dreieckquerlenker, Schraubenfedern, Teleskopstoßdämpfer und Torsionsstabilisator. Hinten Einzelradaufhängung mit gegabelten Führungsarmen, Halbachsen mit je zwei Universalgelenken und Längslenkern sowie je zwei Schraubenfedern mit innenliegenden Teleskopstoßdämpfern. Dies ist in einem leicht demontierbaren Hilfsrahmen zusammengefaßt, der durch Gummiaufhängungen mit der Karosserie verbunden ist.

**BREMSEN**: Zweikreis-Vierradscheibenbremsen mit Bremshilfe, selbstnachstellend.
Handbremse, selbstnachstellend, wirkt mechanisch auf die Hinterräder.

**LENKUNG**: Kugelkreislauflenkung. Verstellbare Lenkradsäule.

**RÄDER UND BEREIFUNG**: 185×15 mit Schlauch. Gegen Aufpreis Speichenräder mit Zentralverschluß.

**KRAFTSTOFFVERSORGUNG**: Zwei elektrische Benzinpumpen. Zwei getrennte Tanks, vom Armaturenbrett aus umschaltbar. Tankinhalt 63 l.

**ELEKTR. AUSRUSTUNG UND INSTRUMENTE**: Wechsestromlichtmaschine, 12-Volt-Anlage, Rückfahrscheinwerfer, Scheibenwischer mit zwei Stufen, Scheibenwaschanlage, Lichthupe, Tourenzähler, Ampèremeter, Uhr, Zigarrenanzünder etc.

**KAROSSERIE**: Selbsttragende Sicherheits-Karosserie, 4-türig, 5 Plätze, Lederpolsterung, Veloursteppiche, vorn und hinten ausklappbare Armlehnen; das Armaturenbrett ist aus poliertem feingemasertem Walnußholz mit abgepolsterten Kanten. Kofferrauminhalt 530 Liter; Reserverad und Werkzeug befinden sich unter dem Kofferraumboden.

**HEIZUNG UND BELUFTUNG**: Frischluft-Heizungssystem für vorn und hinten mit zweistufigem Gebläse. Für die Vordersitze ist diese Anlage getrennt regulierbar.

**HAUPTABMESSUNGEN**: Radstand 273 cm, Spur vorn 141 cm, Spur hinten 137 cm, Länge 477 cm, Breite 170 cm, Höhe 138 cm, Wendekreis 10,2 m.

**The construction program expanded upward in the Sixties to include the 420 series. The cars replaced the venerable Mark IX, built until 1961, at the top of the line. The very wide and flat body was strongly influenced by the Mark II except for the front and rear portions.**

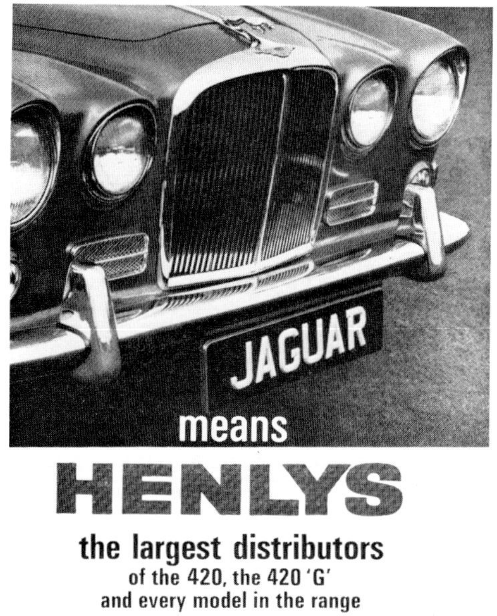


# JAGUAR
420

Fast, stately touring sedan

**MOTOR:** Six-cylinder XK motor with dual overhead cam two carburetors. Compression ratio 8:1, bore 92.07 mm x mm, displacement 4235 cc, 245 HP at 5500 rpm, 39 mkg at Fan control via temperature-dependent viscose coupling.

**GEARS:** Fully synchronized 4-speed gearbox, stick shift. (overdrive) can be switched onto fourth gear by a switch on th column.
Optional fully automatic transmission (Hydraulic torque and 3-speed planetary gears) with two drive areas (D1 D which can be selected at driver's choice.

**SUSPENSION:** Front wishbone transverse links, coil telescopic shock absorbers and torsion stabilizer. Indepen suspension with forked leading arms, half-axles with two joints and longitudinal links each, plus two coil spri telescopic shock absorbers inside. This is contained in demountable subframe which is attached to the body b mounts.

**BRAKES:** Dual-circuit four-wheel disc brakes with servo a self-adjusting. Hand brake, self-adjusting, works mechanica rear wheels.

**STEERING:** Ball-joint steering. Adjustable steering colum

**WHEELS AND TIRES:** 185x15 with tubes. Optional spoke with central hubs.

**FUEL SYSTEM:** Two electric fuel pumps, two separa controlled from dashboard. Tank capacity 63 liters.

**ELECTRIC EQUIPMENT AND INSTRUMENTS:** AC g 12-volt system, back-up light, two-speed windshield wipe shield washer system, flashers, tachometer, ammeter, clock, lighter etc.

**BODYWORK:** Self-supporting safety body, 4 doors, 5 seats upholstery, velour carpets, folding front and rear armrests; ins panel of polished fine-grain walnut wood with padded corner capacity 530 liters, spare wheel and tools located under the space floor.

**HEATING AND VENTILATION:** Fresh-air heating system and rear with two-speed fan. This system is separately control the front seat.

**MAIN DIMENSIONS:** Wheelbase 273 cm, front track 141 track 137 cm, length 477 cm, width 170 cm, height 138 cm, circle 10.2 meters.

## 1966

**The greatest luxury prevailed in the top model, the 420 G, and the 4.2 liter motor provided superior performance in any situation.**

This brochure page is identical to that on page 50 except for the subtitle: 420 G  The great luxury sedan.

# JAGUAR

420 G

Die große Luxus-Limousine

**MOTOR:** Sechszylinder „XK"-Motor mit zwei obenliegenden Nockenwellen und drei Vergasern. Verdichtung 8 : 1, Bohrung 92,07 mm × Hub 106 mm. Zylinderinhalt 4235 ccm, 265 PS bei 5500 U/min. Ventilatorsteuerung über temperaturabhängige Viskosekupplung.

**GETRIEBE:** Vollsynchronisiertes 4-Gang-Getriebe, Knüppelschaltung. Ein Schnellgang (Overdrive) kann durch einen Schalter an der Lenksäule zum vierten Gang zugeschaltet werden.
Gegen Aufpreis vollautomatisches Getriebe (Hydr. Drehmomentwandler und 3-Gang-Planetengetriebe) mit zwei Fahrbereichen (D 1 / D 2), von denen einer wahlweise auch geschaltet werden kann.

**RADAUFHÄNGUNG:** Vorn Trapez-Dreieckquerlenker, Schraubenfedern, Teleskopstoßdämpfer und Torsionsstabilisator. Hinten Einzelradaufhängung mit gegabelten Führungsarmen, Halbachsen mit je zwei Universalgelenken und Längslenkern sowie je zwei Schraubenfedern mit innenliegenden Teleskopstoßdämpfern. Dies ist in einem leicht demontierbaren Hilfsrahmen zusammengefaßt, der durch Gummiaufhängungen mit der Karosserie verbunden ist.

**BREMSEN:** Zweikreis-Vierradscheibenbremsen mit Bremshilfe, selbstnachstellend.
Handbremse, selbstnachstellend, wirkt mechanisch auf die Hinterräder.

**LENKUNG:** „Varamatic", Servolenkung mit progressiver Wirkung. 2,75 Umdrehungen von Anschlag zu Anschlag. Verstellbare Lenkradsäule.

**RÄDER UND BEREIFUNG:** Preßstahlfelgen 205×14 mit Schlauch.

**KRAFTSTOFFVERSORGUNG:** Zwei elektrische Benzinpumpen. Zwei getrennte Tanks, vom Armaturenbrett aus umschaltbar. Tankinhalt 91 l.

**ELEKTR. AUSRUSTUNG UND INSTRUMENTE:** Wechsestromlichtmaschine, 12-Volt-Anlage, Rückfahrscheinwerfer, Scheibenwischer mit zwei Stufen, Scheibenwaschanlage, Lichthupe, Tourenzähler, Amperemeter, Uhr, Zigarrenanzünder etc.

**KAROSSERIE:** Selbsttragende Sicherheits-Karosserie, 4-türig, 5 Plätze, perforierte Lederpolsterung, Velourteppiche, vorn und hinten ausklappbare Armlehnen; das Armaturenbrett ist aus poliertem feingemasertem Walnußholz mit abgepolsterten Kanten. Kofferrauminhalt 750 Liter; Reserverad und Werkzeug befinden sich rechts im Kofferraum.

**HEIZUNG UND BELÜFTUNG:** Frischluft-Heizungssystem für vorn und hinten mit zweistufigem Gebläse. Für die Vordersitze ist diese Anlage getrennt regulierbar.

**HAUPTABMESSUNGEN:** Radstand 305 cm, Spur vorn 147 cm, Spur hinten 147 cm, Länge 513 cm, Breite 193 cm, Höhe 138 cm, Wendekreis 11,3 m.

# 240/340: Belt-tightening—but with Taste

In 1967 there was no more Mark II, but the car lived on. And, to be sure, in the form of the 240 or 340. They represented the thrifty versions of the Mark II, but were scarcely inferior to their ancestors in quality or character. The two types remained in Jaguar's program until 1968 and 1969 respectively. Among Jaguar fans, they are also ranked in the "Mark Two" concept, even though they were no longer called that by the factory. They were also produced only in comparatively small numbers—see page 92.

The Model 240, with the world-famous XK motor with dual overhead camshafts, which has brought Jaguars victory after victory on the racetracks of the world—including five record victories at Le Mans—offers many new refinements in styling, performance and technical features.

The new version of the 2.4 liter XK motor for the Jaguar 240 develops no less than 133 HP now, and is fitted with the cylinder head that is also used in the E-Type GT cars, plus S.U. dual carburetors and dual exhaust systems.

This model is available with fully synchronized four-speed transmission with or without overdrive, or with the Borg-Warner 35 automatic transmission with torque converter. Standard equipment includes disc brakes with servo assistance on all four wheels, dashboard with many instruments, highly effective heating and defrosting system, two-speed windshield wipers and electric windshield washing system.

In its technical perfection and luxurious amenities this model represents the Jaguar tradition of high performance with high quality.

**In September of 1967 the Mark II types appeared in reworked form, designated 240 and 340, the version with 3.8 liter motor was no longer available.**

In the wide and deep luggage compartment you can easily stow 382 liters of luggage for 5 people. It is completely lined and illuminated in the dark. Spare wheel and tools are located in a well under the luggage compartment.

**Externally there was scarcely a change, but the interior equipment had undergone an unfortunate thinning. One now sat on imitation leather seats, and the hardwood of the numerous panels had given way to artificial materials.**

LHP 240F

## luxus und bequemlichkeit für fahrer und passagiere.

Das Innere des 240 Fünfsitzer-Limousine soll grösste Bequemlichkeit bei höchstem Luxus vermitteln, die im Verein mit dem leisen, mühelosen Lauf des Modelles selbst längste Reisen zu einem vollkommenen Vergnügen machen.

Die Einzelvordersitze, die sich in der Höhe und im Abstand verstellen lassen, und die geräumige hintere Sitzbank mit rückklappbarer Armstütze in der Mitte sind mit weichem Schaumgummi gepolstert und verschwenderisch überzogen.

Der gesamte Wagenboden ist mit Teppichen belegt.

Die zahlreichen Instrumente sind in einem schönen Armaturenbrett untergebracht, das wie alle Holzteile aus poliertem Nussholz besteht. Die leistungsstarke Frischluftheizung und das Defrostersystem schliessen eine getrennte Heizleitung in den hinteren Teil des Wagens ein.

## luxury and comfort for driver and passengers

The interior of the 240 five-seater sedan is meant to provide the greatest comfort with the highest luxury, which, together with the quiet running of the model, make even the longest trips a thoroughgoing pleasure.

The individual front seats, which can be adjusted in height and distance, and the roomy rear seat bench with a folding armrest in the middle, are upholstered with soft foam rubber and lavishly covered. The whole floor of the car is covered with carpeting.

The numerous instruments are set in a nice instrument panel that, like all wooden parts, consists of polished walnut wood. The high-performance fresh-air heater and the defroster system include a separate heating system in the rear part of the car.

**Despite such thriftiness, it was still a pleasure to glide along in a Jaguar, for the combination of luxury and sportiness was scarcely to be found elsewhere in this form.**

**The motors had received new cylinder heads, which provided a light increase in performance. Even the small 240 motor mpressed with its swift running and good elasticity.**

he Jaguar XK motor is known all over the world as a perfect xpression of technical performance potential. It includes everything at is worth striving for in the present-day state of technical progress building auto motors. The dual overhead camshafts work directly n the valves, which are dropped at a 70-degree angle in the emispherical combustion chambers housed in the high-performance luminum cylinder head. The well-balanced massive crankshaft is ounted in seven unusually large bearings of 2.75-inch diameter. hus quiet running is provided over an extraordinarily large spectrum f engine speed. In every phase of construction and assembly, the most tringent tests are applied. *Every* motor is tested precisely on the test ench. In the whole world there is no motor that has gained a better eputation for durability and 100% reliability under all conditions an the Jaguar XK motor. It has become the standard by which other ar motors are measured.
hown is the 2.4 liter motor of the Jaguar 240. Displacement 2485 cc, 33 BHP at 5500 rpm.

Der Jaguar XK Motor wird auf der ganzen Welt als perfekter Ausdruck technischer Leistungsfähigkeit anerkannt. Er enthält alles, was beim heutigen Stand der fortschrittlichen Technik bei der Konstruktion von Automotoren erstrebenswert ist. Die beiden obenliegenden Nockenwellen wirken direkt auf die Ventile, die in einem Winkel von 70° in die halbkugelförmigen Verbrennungskammern hängen, die in dem Hochleistungszylinderkopf aus Aluminium untergebracht sind. Die gut ausgewogene massive Kurbelwelle ist auf sieben ungewöhnlich grossen Lagern von 2 3/4 Zoll Durchmesser gelagert. Damit ist ruehiger Lauf im ausserordentlich weiten Drehzahlbereich des Motors gegeben. In jeder Phase der Herstellung und des Zusammenbaus werden die strengsten Prüfungen vorgenommen. *Jeder* Motor wird genau auf dem Prüfstand getestet. Es gibt auf der ganzen Welt keinen Motor, der sich einen besseren Ruf für Langlebigkeit und hundertprozentige Verlässlichkeit unter allen Bedingungen erworben hätte, als der Jaguar XK Motor. Er wurde zum Masstab, nach dem andere Automotoren beurteilt werden.
Abgebildet der 2,4 Liter Motor des Jaguar 240. Hubraum 2485 ccm, 133 Brems PS bei 5500 U/m

# einzelheiten des modelles Jaguar 240

- Ganzstahlkarosserie, vier Türen, Limousine mit fünf Sitzen, rahmenlose Bauart, Maximalsteifheit bei Minimalgewicht.
- Karosserie rost- und schallsicher durch neueste Fertigungstechnik.
- Inneres luxuriös und reichhaltig ausgestattet.
- Geräumiger Kofferaum mit 380 l Inhalt.
- Hochleistungs-Heiz- und Defrostsystem mit getrennter Heizleitung in dem hinteren Teil des Wagens.
- Reichhaltige Instrumentierung, u.a. Geschwindigkeitsmesser, Drehzahlmesser, elektrische Uhr, Amperemeter, öldruckanzeige, Wassertemperaturanzeige, Benzinuhr, kombiniertes Warnlicht für angezogene Handbremse und Bremsflüssigkeitsstand.
- Elektrische Ausrüstung, u.a. Rückfahrscheinwerfer, Kartenleselampe, Armaturenbrettbeleuchtung für zwei Leuchtstärken, Zweiblattscheibenwischer mit zwei Geschwindigkeiten, Doppelscheibenwascher, Zigarrenanzünder.
- Wahl zwischen Vollsynchron-Vierganggetriebe mit oder ohne Overdrive oder Vollautomatik mit Drehmomentwandler.
- Scheibenbremsen mit Servohilfe an allen Rädern.
- Jaguar-Konstruktion mit unabhängiger Vorderradaufhängung und Halbachse hinten.
- Kugelumlauflenkung für höchste Präzision. Gegen Aufpreis Servolenkung erhältlich.
- Befestigungspunkte für Sicherheitsgürtel in die Karosserie eingebaut.
- Reichhaltiges Werkzeug in einem besonderen Behälter.

**Details of the Model 240 Jaguar**
All-steel body, four-door sedan with five seats, no-frame construction, maximum rigidity with minimum weight.
Body is rust- and scale-free thanks to a new manufacturing technique.

Luxurious and lavish interior furnishing.

Roomy trunk with 380 liter capacity.

High-performance heater and defroster system with separate heater ducts to the rear part of the car.

Numerous instruments including speedometer, tachometer, electric clock, ammeter, oil pressure and water temperature gauges, fuel gauge, combined warning light for hand brake and brake fluid.

Electric equipment includes back-up light, map-reading lamp, two-stage instrument panel light, two-speed dual windshield wipers, dual windshield washers, cigarette lighter.

Choice of fully synchronized four-speed transmission with or without overdrive or fully automatic with torque converter.

Disc brakes with servo assistance on all four wheels.

Jaguar construction with independent front suspension and rear half-shafts.
Ball-joint steering for highest precision. Servo assistance available optionally.

Attachment points for seat belts built into the body.
Ample tools in a special case.

**On the basis of its sporting characteristics, the Mark II became a desirable competition car in the touring car class. Many firms specialized in enhancing the Jaguar's performance, and the merciless duels with their arch-rivals, the Mercedes-Benz 300 SE, are unforgettable.**

**Right page: Nürburgring duel: Eugen Böhringer versus Peter Lindner, who was not only one of the most capable representatives of the Jaguar cause when it was a question of sales, but also showed in numerous races what the wildcats of Coventry were capable of. Lindner was a dedicated racing driver a lost his life much too early.**

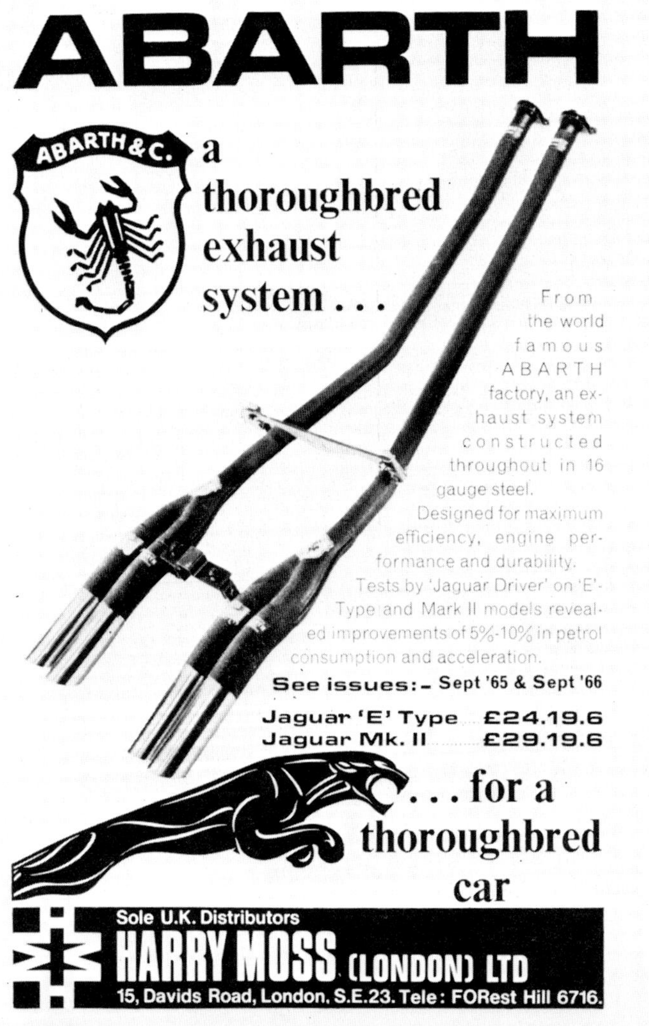

S-PD 703

WI-PL 1

D
WI
PL 1

# Daimler V8 alias Jaguar

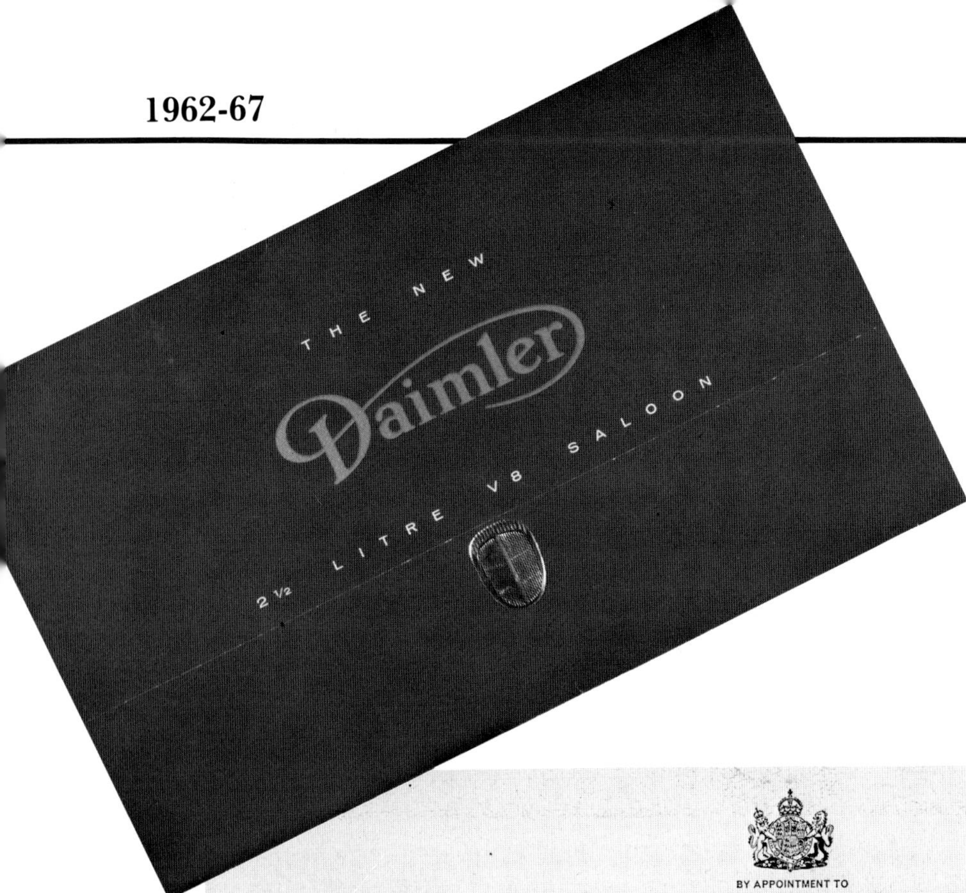


When Jaguar took over the faltering firm of Daimler—one of England's oldest automobile manufacturers!—it received the added reward of a splendid V8 motor. It fit perfectly into the Jaguar Mark II, creating a new exclusive model. The British have been creating combinations of this kind for years. The Daimler V8 2.5 Liter was a sporty four-door sedan for ambitious connoisseurs.

BY APPOINTMENT TO
H.M. QUEEN ELIZABETH THE QUEEN MOTHER
MOTOR CAR MANUFACTURERS
THE DAIMLER CO. LTD.

Seit jeher bürgt das Prestige der Marke „Daimler" für einen besonders hohen Qualitäts- und Leistungsstandard. Die neue „Daimler" 2,5 l V8 Limousine setzt diese getreulich gewahrte Tradition in modernem Sinne fort.

Der bewährte 2,5 l V8 Motor — von dem die Fachzeitschrift „The Motor" die „außergewöhnliche Drehmomentleistung und turbinengleiche Elastizität, welche in einem überraschend weiten Geschwindigkeitsbereich vorhanden ist", besonders hervorhebt — verleiht diesem Wagen gleichermaßen hervorragende Fahreigenschaften, ob er nun mit der erzielbaren Spitzengeschwindigkeit von 180 km/h oder in den unteren Bereichen gefahren wird.

Der neue „Daimler" ist serienmäßig mit einem Borg-Warner Automatik-Getriebe neuester Bauart ausgestattet, welches die Annehmlichkeiten einer Vollautomatik mit den wichtigen Vorzügen einer manuellen Schaltung, nämlich volle Motorbremswirkung in den einzelnen Bereichen, aufweist.

Die luxuriöse, bis ins kleinste Detail durchdachte Innenausstattung bietet Fahrer und Passagieren echten „Daimler"-Komfort, und somit prägt ein Optimum an Leistung, Sicherheit und Eleganz dieses neue „Daimler"-Modell zu einem exklusiven Spitzenfahrzeug, das selbst in der Weltelite eine Sonderstellung einnimmt.

For many years the prestige of the Daimler marque has guaranteed a particularly high quality and performance. The new Daimler 2.5 liter V8 sedan embodies this loyally maintained tradition in the modern sense.

The proven 2.5 liter V8 motor—of which the specialist magazine "The Motor" particularly stressed the "extraordinary torque and turbine-like flexibility that are available in a remarkably wide range of engine speeds"—gives this car equally outstanding driving qualities, whether it is driven at the attainable top speed of 180 kph or at lower speeds.

The new Daimler has a Borg-Warner automatic transmission of the newest type as standard equipment, which combines the convenience of an automatic with the important advantages of a manual transmission, namely full motor braking effect in the various areas.

The luxurious interior decor, refined to the smallest detail, offers driver and passengers true Daimler comfort, thus attaining the optimum performance, safety and elegance and making this new Daimler model an exclusive top-line automobile that takes a special place even among the world's elite.

In 1960 Jaguar had already bought up the debt-ridden Daimler firm and thus obtained a wonderful V-eight-cylinder motor, which was installed in the Mark II as of November 1962. The thus ennobled car was given the impressive name of Daimler 2 1/2 Litre Saloon, a particularly refined interior decor, and a typical ribbed radiator grille with a large D as the emblem of Daimler.

THE MODERN PRESTIGE CAR

The lively golden D on the hub of the steering wheel indicates that this instrument panel belongs to a Daimler, a car that was made in much smaller numbers than the better-known Mark II, which gave it then, as now, great exclusivity.

**INSTRUMENTENANORDNUNG AM ARMATURENBRETT**

1. *Ampèremeter*
2. *Benzinanzeiger*
3. *Hauptlichtschalter*
4. *Öldruckmesser*
5. *Kühlwasserthermometer*
6. *Tourenzähler*
7. *Elektrische Uhr*
8. *Kilometerzähler*
9. *Choke*
10. *Choke Warnlicht*
11. *Schalter für Innenbeleuchtung*
12. *Schalter für Instrumentenbeleuchtung (zweistufig)*
13. *Schalter für Heizungsgebläse (zweistufig)*
14. *Zündschalter*
15. *Zigarrenanzünder*
16. *Starterknopf*
17. *Lichtschalter für Kartenleselampe*
18. *Elektrischer Scheibenwischer (zweistufig)*
19. *Schalter für elektrische Scheibenwaschanlage*
20. *Automatik-Gangwahlhebel*
21. *Uhrzeigereinstellknopf*
22. *Scheinwerferabblendschalter*
23. *Hornring*
24. *Kontrollicht für Blinker und Automatik*
25. *Tageszählereinstellknopf*
26. *Blinkerhebel*
27. *Heizungsregulierhebel (Temperatur)*
28. *Heizungsregulierhebel (Luftstrom)*
29. *Bedienungsknopf für Radio (falls montiert)*
30. *Bedienungsknopf für Radio (falls montiert)*
31. *Radioverkleidung (falls montiert)*
32. *Hebel für Stirnwandventilationsklappe*
33. *Kontrollicht für Bremsflüssigkeitsstand und Handbremse*

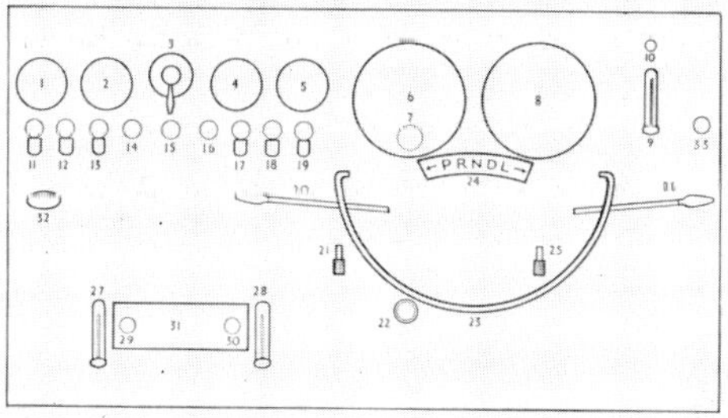

The outstanding sign of the Daimler 2.5 liter V8 motor is its extremely quiet running and turbine-like evenness.
It produces 142 HP at 5500 rpm, and its remarkable elasticity allows driving the car at 15 kph in direct gear and accelerating gently and quickly from this speed without a trace of hesitation.

## NSTRUMENT ARRANGEMENT )N THE DASHBOARD

Ammeter
Fuel gauge
Main light switch
Oil pressure gauge
Water thermometer
Tachometer
Electric clock
Odometer
Choke
Choke warning light
Interior light switch
Dasgboard light switch
Heater fan switch (2-speed)
Ignition lock
Cigarette lighter
Starter button
Map reading light switch

18. Windshield wiper switch (2-speed)
19. Windshield washer switch
20. Automatic shift lever
21. Clock setting control
22. Headlight dimmer switch
23. Horn ring
24. Flasher indicator light
25. Daily odometer control
26. Directional light lever
27. Heater control (temperature)
28. Heater control (airstream)
29. Radio control knob (if installed)
30. Radio control knob (if installed)
31. Radio cover (if installed)
32. Ventilator control
33. Brake fluid and hand brake indicator light

ery instrument on the polished walnut instrument panel is located ectly in the driver's field of vision and is easy to read. All operating ers are practically arranged and easy to reach. Switches and truments are clearly lettered and indirectly lit. If the radio is not talled as an optional extra then the opening for it is covered by a ther panel.

Otherwise almost identical to the Mark II, the Daimler had a silky soft V8 motor under its hood which, combined with Borg Warner automatic transmission (standard), guaranteed swift and very dependable movement.

URG 690

Likewise staying in production under Jaguar's direction: the conservative big Daimler Majestic sedan, which was also built with lengthened wheelbase and ordered in this form as limousines for formal occasions.

Likewise taken over by Jaguar was this oddly styled sports roadster, which had made its debut in New York in 1959. Under the polyester body was the V8 motor developed by Daimler. The car remained an outsider, as not everybody could feel attracted to the somewhat overdone body styling.

Daimler V8. 3997 of these cars were built—in contrast to the Jaguar, most of them stayed in England.

# TECHNICAL DATA

MOTOR: V8 machine, two banks of four cylinders each forming a 90-degree angle, 76.2 mm bore, 69.85 mm stroke, displacement 2548 cc. Power 142 HP at 5500 rpm. Compression ratio 8.2:1, overhead valves activated by pushrods and a central camshaft, 2 S.U. H.D.6 downdraft carburetors and dual exhaust system. Water circulation cooling with pump and radiator, regulated by thermostat in tributary. Pressure lubrication by oil pump in the oilpan and built-in mainstream oil filter. Cast iron cylinder block. Cylinder head of high-tensile aluminum alloy with hemispherical combustion chambers. Pistons of aluminum alloy. Steel connecting rods.

**TRANSMISSION:** Fully automatic Borg-Warner transmission of Type 35 with oil cooler. Gear sleector lever on the steering column. Gear ratios: Low gear 21.75/10.87, middle gear 13.20/6.60, direct gear 9.10/4.55. Reverse gear 19.02/9.51.

**SUSPENSION:** Independent front suspension with wishbone transverse links and coil springs with hydraulic telescopic shock absorbers. Rear suspension by semi-elliptic leaf springs and longitudinal links plus hydraulic telescopic shock absorbers.

**BRAKES:** Dunlop disc brakes with quick-change pads on all four wheels. Servo brake assistance, hand brake with automatic adjustment. Set hand brake indicated by warning light on the instrument panel, which also serves as brake fluid warning light.

**STEERING:** Burman ball-joint steering with telescopically adjustable two-spoke steering wheel of 43 cm diameter. Optional leftor right-hand steering. 4.7 revolutions from block to block. Turning circle 10.5 meters. Power steering is available as an optional extra.

**WHEELS AND TIRES:** Pressed steel disc wheels with lug bolts. Dunlop RS 5 6.40 x 15 tires with tubes. Spare wheel and tire.

**FUEL SYSTEM:** Electric S.U. fuel pump. Tank capacity 54 liters.

**ELECTRICAL EQUIPMENT AND INSTRUMENTS:** Lucas 12-volt battery (capacity 51 A/st after 10 h norm) with combined voltage regulator. Air-cooled generator. Side lights built into upper part of fenders, with ruby glass reflectors visible to driver as indicators of light functioning. Headlights with asymmetrical dimmer and foot-operated dimmer switch. Horn ring on the steering column. Rear license plate light. Automatically activated flasher with indicator light. Instruments and lettered control switches indirectly lighted, controlled by a two-stage switch. Shaded map-reading light on the lower dashboard frame. Dual interior lights on the middle door pillars as well as one over the rear window can be activated by a switch on the instrument panel or



# TECHNISCHE DATEN

**MOTOR:** V8 Maschine, je 4 Zylinder im 90°-Winkel, 76,2 mm Bohrung, 69,85 mm Hub, Hubraum 2.548 ccm. Leistung 142 PS bei 5.500 U/min. Kompressionsverhältnis 8,2 : 1, obenliegende, durch Stößel und eine zentrale Nockenwelle gesteuerte Ventile, 2 S.U. Fallstromvergaser H.D. 6 und doppelte Auspuffanlage. Durch Thermostat im Nebenfluß geregelte Wasserumlaufkühlung mit Pumpe und Ventilator. Druckschmierung durch in der Ölwanne befindliche Ölpumpe und eingebauten Hauptstromölfilter. Zylinderblock aus Gußeisen. Zylinderkopf aus hochdehnbarer Aluminiumlegierung mit halbkugelförmigen Verbrennungsräumen. Kolben aus Aluminiumlegierung. Stahlpleuelstangen.

**KRAFTÜBERTRAGUNG:** Vollautomatisches Borg-Warner-Getriebe vom Typ 35 mit Ölkühler. Gangwahlhebel an der Lenksäule. Übersetzungsverhältnisse: Niederer Gang 21,75/10,87, mittlerer Gang 13,20/6,60, direkter Gang 9,10/4,55. Retourgang 19,02/9,51.

**AUFHÄNGUNG:** Unabhängige Vorderradaufhängung mit Trapez-Dreiecksquerlenkern und Schraubenfedern mit hydraulischen Teleskopstoßdämpfern. Hinterradaufhängung mit halbelliptischen Cantilever-Federn und Längslenkern sowie hydraulischen Teleskopstoßdämpfern.

**BREMSEN:** Dunlop-Scheibenbremsen mit rasch auswechselbaren Belägen an allen vier Rädern. Servo-Bremshilfe, Handbremse mit automatischer Nachstellung. Angezogene Handbremse wird durch ein Warnlicht am Armaturenbrett, welches auch als Warnlicht für den Bremsflüssigkeitsstand dient, angezeigt.

**LENKUNG:** Burman-Kugelumlauflenkung mit teleskopisch verstellbarem Zweispeichenlenkrad von 43 cm Durchmesser. Wahlweise Links- oder Rechtssteuerung. 4,7 Umdrehungen von Anschlag zu Anschlag. Wendekreis 10,5 m. Als wahlweises Extra ist Servolenkung erhältlich.

**RÄDER UND BEREIFUNG:** Preßstahlscheibenräder mit Bolzenbefestigung. Dunlop-RS 5-Reifen 6,40 x 15 mit Schläuchen. Reserverad und Reifen.

**TREIBSTOFFZUFUHR:** Elektrische S.U. Benzinpumpe. Tankinhalt 54 Liter.

**ELEKTRISCHE AUSRÜSTUNG UND INSTRUMENTE:** Lucas-12-Volt-Batterie (Kapazität 51 A/st nach 10 h Norm) mit kombiniertem Spannungsregler. Luftgekühlte Lichtmaschine. Seitenleuchten im oberen Teil der Kotflügel eingebaut, mit Rubinglasreflektoren zur Funktionskontrolle der Birnen für den Fahrer sichtbar. Scheinwerfer mit asymmetrischem Abblendlicht und mit fußbetätigtem Abblendschalter, Lichthupenhebel an der Lenksäule. Doppelte Nebellampen. Separates Schluß-Stop-Licht sowie Blinker und Reflektor in einer Einheit. Rückfahrscheinwerfer. Hintere Kennzeichenbeleuchtung. Automatisch ausschaltende Blinker mit Kontrollicht. Instrumente und beschriftete Bedienungsschalter indirekt beleuchtet, durch einen zweistufigen Abblendschalter zu betätigen. Abgeschirmte Kartenleselampe an der unteren Instrumentenbrettleiste. Doppelte Innenlichter an den mittleren Türpfosten sowie eines über dem Rückfenster können sowohl durch einen Schalter am Instrumentenbrett als auch automatisch beim

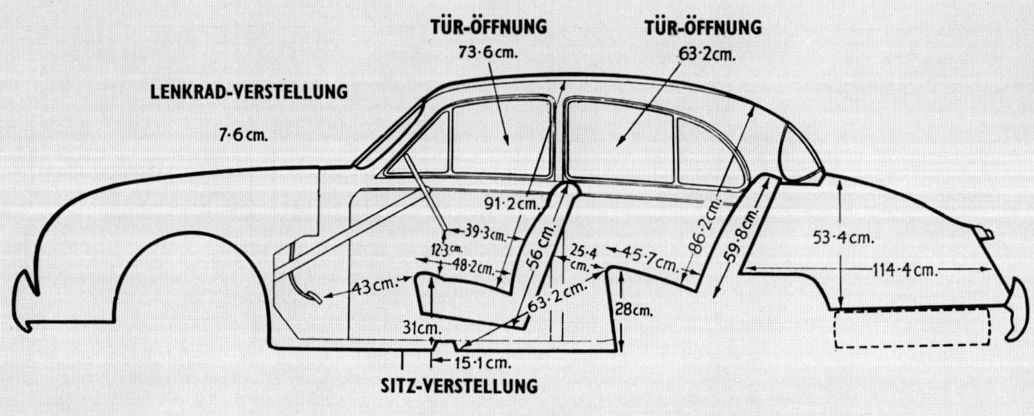

Öffnen einer jeden der vier Türen betätigt werden. Zigarrenanzünder mit Leuchtsockel. Doppeltonhorn. Doppelte Scheibenwischer mit zwei Geschwindigkeiten sowie automatischer Ruhestellungsarretierung. Elektrischer Scheibenwascher. Startermotor. Automatische Zündverstellung durch Vakuum und Fliehkraftregler. Zündspule im Ölbad. Kilometerzähler, 127 mm im Durchmesser. Elektrisch betriebener Tourenzähler mit elektrischer Uhr, 127 mm im Durchmesser. Ampèremeter. Elektrischer Öldruckmesser, Kühlwasserthermometer, Benzinuhr mit Warnlicht, kombiniertes Warnlicht für Handbremse und Bremsflüssigkeitsstand.

**KAROSSERIE:** Viertürige, fünfsitzige Ganzstahlkarosserie. Selbsttragende Chassiskonstruktion, welche trotz minimalem Gewicht höchste Verwindungsfestigkeit aufweist. Große Panoramawindschutzscheibe sowie schmale Seitenpfosten und großes, bombiertes Heckfenster gewähren beste Rundsicht. Die bombierte Windschutzscheibe behindert in keiner Weise den leichten Ein- und Ausstieg. Großer, blendfrei einstellbarer Rückspiegel. Verchromte Fensterrahmen an allen Türen. Spezial-Druckknopfschnallen, welche so konstruiert sind, daß sie im Winter nicht einfrieren können. Chromzierleisten an den Regenrinnen und entlang der Karosserieseitenwand. Mit feinstem Vaumol-Leder überzogene dicke Schaumgummipolsterung. Die vorderen Sitze sind geteilt und einzeln verstellbar, mit einer zusätzlichen Verstellungsmöglichkeit auf Reichweite und Sitzwinkel. Instrumentenbrett aus feingemasertem, poliertem Nußholz, mit Kilometerzähler und Tourenzähler im direkten Blickfeld des Fahrers und separaten Instrumenten, wie Öldruckmesser, Kühlwasserthermometer, Benzinuhr und Ampèremeter. Auf der Mitfahrerseite befindet sich ein versperrbares, automatisch beleuchtetes Handschuhfach. Einbaumöglichkeit für Radio und Lautsprecher. Zweispeichenlenkrad mit halbrundem Hornring. Vorder- und Hintertüren sind mit großen Seitentaschen und Armlehnen versehen. Die hinteren seitlichen Armstützen sind mit Aschenbechern ausgestattet. Innere schwenkbare Sonnenblenden. Qualitätsteppiche über dicken Filzunterlagen. Starke, um die Kanten der Karosserie gezogene Stoßstangen mit Ziernasen. Verchromte Türschlösser. Befestigungsvorrichtungen für vordere und hintere Sicherheitsgurte.

**HEIZUNG UND KLIMAANLAGE:** Hochleistungsheizungsanlage mit Defroster für die Windschutzscheibe. Ventilator mit zwei Geschwindigkeiten, durch einen Schalter am Instrumentenbrett einstellbar.

**RESERVERAD UND WERKZEUG:** Das Reserverad ist in einem separaten Fach unterhalb des Kofferraumes leicht zugänglich untergebracht. Eine spezielle, komplett ausgerüstete Werkzeugkassette ist ebenfalls im Reservefach untergebracht. Wagenheber und Radmutternschlüssel befinden sich im Kofferraum.

**WAGENHEBER:** Hinten und vorne beidseitig der Karosserie vorgesehene Ansatzpunkte ermöglichen ein leichtes Anbringen des Wagenhebers und ein Hochwinden des Wagens mit minimalem Kraftaufwand.

**HAUPTABMESSUNGEN:** Radstand 2,73 m, vordere Spur 1,40 m, hintere Spur 1,36 m, Gesamtlänge 4,59 m, Gesamtbreite 1,70 m, Gesamthöhe 1,46 m, Bodenabstand 0,18 m.

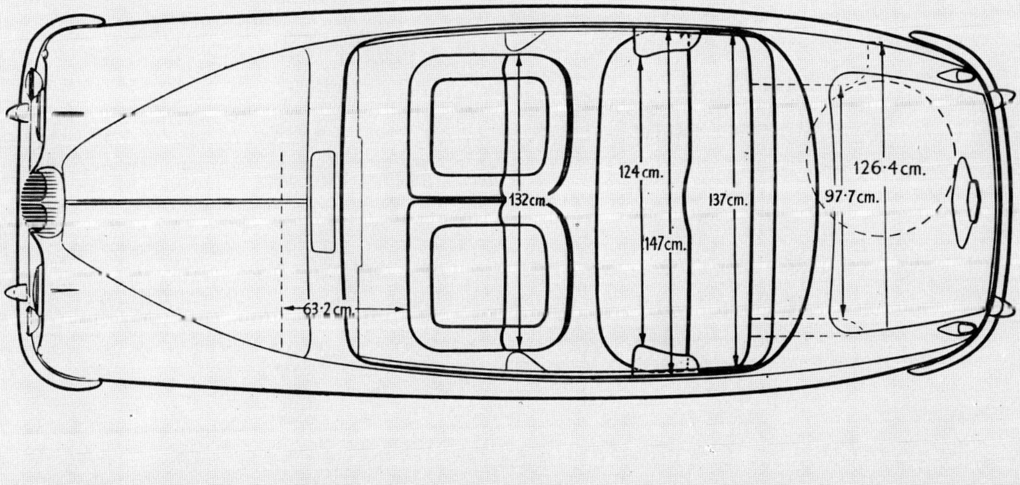


automatically by opening one of the four doors. Cigarette lighter with glowing socket. Two-tone horn. Dual windshield wipers with two speeds and automatic return when stopped. Electric windshield washer. Starter motor. Automatic ignition control by vacuum and flow regulator. Coil in oil bath. Speedometer, 127 mm in diameter. Electrically driven tachometer with electric clock, 127 mm in diameter. Ammeter. Electric oil pressure gauge, water thermometer, fuel gauge with warning light, combined hand brake and brake fluid warning light.

**BODYWORK:** Four-door, five-seat all-steel body. Self-supporting chassis construction, which provides greatest rigidity despite lowest weight. Large panoramic windshield, slim pillars and large bowed rear window guarantee best panoramic view. The bowed windshield in no way interferes with easy entry and exit. Large glare-free adjustable rear-view mirror. Chromed window frames on all doors. Special push-button locks constructed so that they cannot freeze in winter. Chrome ornamental strips on the rain gutters and along the sidewalls of the body. Thick foam rubber upholstery covered with finest Vaumol leather. The front seats are separate and individually adjustable, with additional adjustment possibilities for reach and seat angle. Instrument panel of fine-grained, polished walnut wood, with odometer and tachometer in the driver's direct field of vision and separate instruments, such as oil pressure gauge, water thermometer, fuel gauge and ammeter. On the passenger's side is a locking, automatically lighted glove compartment. Possibility of installing a radio and loudspeaker. Two-spoke steering wheel with semicircular horn ring, front and rear doors equipped with large side pockets and armrests. The rear side armrests are equipped with ashtrays. Adjustable interior sun visors. Quality carpets over thick felt underlays. Strong wrap-around bumpers with decorative overriders. Chromed door locks. Attachment points for front and rear seat belts.

**HEATING AND AIR CONDITIONING:** High-performance heater with defroster for the windshield. Two-speed fan, controlled by a switch on the dashboard.

**SPARE WHEEL AND TOOLS:** The spare wheel is readily available in a separate well under the luggage compartment. A special, completely equipped tool kit is likewise stowed in the spare wheel well. Auto jack and lug nut are found in the luggage compartment.

**AUTO JACK:** At back and front on both sides of the body, attachment points are provided, allowing easy application of the jack and high jacking of the car with a minimum of effort.

**MAIN DIMENSIONS:** Wheelbase 2.73 meters, front track 1.40 meters, rear track 1.36 meters, overall length 4.59 meters, overall width 1.70 meters, overall height 1.46 meters, ground clearance 0.18 meter.

No great headlines or advertising slogans were needed to display the qualities of the Daimler. The model name told the connoisseur everything. And the sales catalog for the V8 was directed only at connoisseurs. Inside too, the catalog was respectably restrained—in the typical English manner of understatement.

# Der Daimler V8-250

Vom ersten Augenblick an hat der Daimler Zweieinhalbliter auf einzigartige Weise das Gefühl luxuriösen Autofahrens vermittelt. Einzigartig durch seinen V8-2,5 Liter Motor mit Doppelvergaser und der Laufruhe einer Turbine; die Aufhängung (Einzelrad Aufhängung vorne, starrachse Hinten), die hervorrgagend bequemes und kontrolliertes Fahren garantiert; die selbstverstärkenden Scheibenbremsen an allen Rädern, die überaus leicht zu betätigen und kraftvoll sind. Zu all dem kommt noch die Standardausstattung hinzu: verstellbare Vordersitze, ventilierte Lederpolsterung, gepolsterte Armaturenbrettkante, beheiztes Heckfenster, Drehstromlichtmaschine, neue, rundgeführte Stosstangen und neue Radzierkappen. Der V8-250 ist in der Tat ein Auto mit sehr individuellem Charakter, ein Auto, das hohe Leistung mit traditionellem Daimler-Komfort und Detailausarbeitung verbindet. Es bietet Prestigewert moderner Art in einem unerreichten Grad. Erhältlich mit Borg-Warner Automatik mit Drehmomentwandler oder mit Viergang-Vollsynchrongetriebe und Overdrive.

**The Britons always knew what they owed their customers, including those on the Continent. Namely the continuation of the English awareness of tradition. One did not photograph a Jaguar or Daimler in the city, on the motorway, or in the parking lot, but before the door of a fine villa.**

**The Daimler V8—250SZ 05**

From the first moment on, the Daimler two and a half liter expresses the feeling of luxurious auto driving in its own inimitable way. Unique for its V8 2.5 liter motor with double carburetor and the quiet running of a turbine; the suspension (independent front suspension, rigid rear axle), that guarantees outstandingly comfortable and controlled driving; the self-strengthening disc brakes on all wheels, which are also easy to apply and powerful. Along with all that, there is also the standard equipment: adjustable front seats, venilated leather upholstery, padded dashboard edges, heated rear window, alternating current generator, new rounded bumpers and new ornamental hubcaps. The V8-250 is indeed a car with a very individual character, a car that blends high-performance with traditional Daimler comfort and meticulousness. It offers modern-day prestige value to an unequaled degree. Available with Borg-Warner automobile transmission with torque convertor or with fully synchronized four-speed gearbox and overdrive.

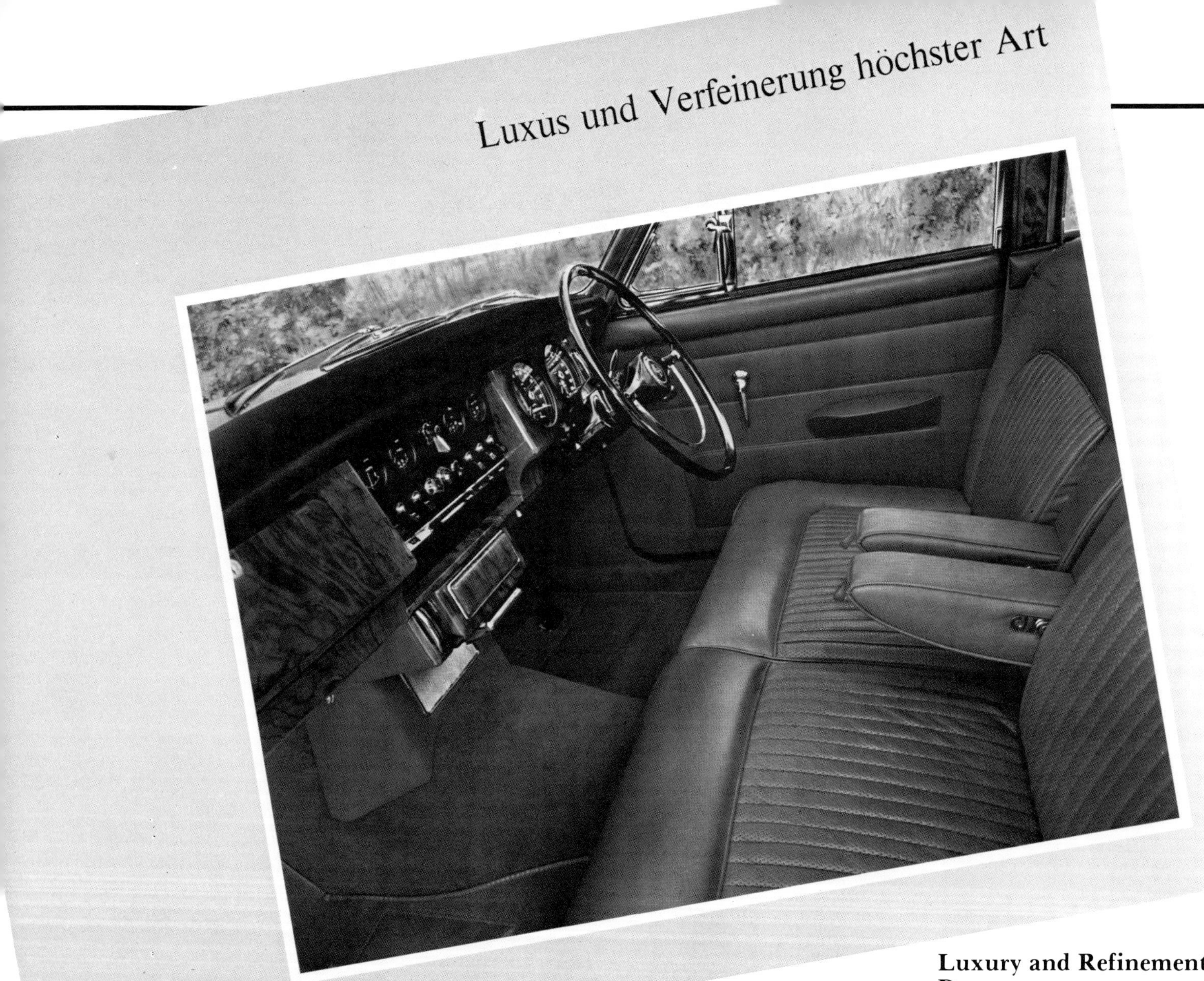


**Luxury and Refinement of the Highest Degree**

**The seats of a Daimler were naturally always covered with fine leather, and the finest walnut veneers were chosen for the dashboard and the wooden panels of the doors and window frames.**

**Even if it was not the most powerful of the motors that were built into the Mark II, the Daimler V8 motor was certainly the most cultivated powerplant of this series.**

## The Famous Daimler 2.5 Liter V8 Motor

The Daimler 2.5 liter V8 motor, which was described by "The Motor" as "extraordinary in terms of its torque and its turbinelike quietness of running over an unbelievably great range of speed . . .", develops 140 brake horsepower at 5800 rpm. Because of its astounding elasticity, the car can be driven in top gear at only 15 kph and yet accelerated quickly and without hesitation. This V8 motor was carefully constructed through and through—with a care that has made the name "Daimler" a sign of quality all over the world.

## Der berühmte Daimler 2,5 Liter V8 Motor

Der Daimler 2,5 Liter V8 Motor, der von „Motor“ als „aussergewöhnlich in Hinblick auf sein Drehmoment und auf seine turbinenähnliche Laufruhe über einen unglaublich grossen Drehzahlbereich . . .“ bezeichnet wurde, entwickelt 140 Brems-PS bei 5800 U/m. Aufgrund seiner erstaunlichen Elastizität kann der Wagen im höchsten Gang mit nur 15 Stundenkilometern gefahren und doch ruckfrei und schnell beschleunigt werden. Dieser V8 Motor wurde durch und durch sorgfältig konstruiert — mit einer Sorgfalt, die den Namen „Daimler“ auf der ganzen Welt zu einer Qualitätsmarke gemacht hat.

## Für äusserste Verlässlichkeit gewählt . . . überall

Dem Mann, der seinen Wagen täglich bei allen vorstellbaren Fahrbedingungen verwendet, bietet der Daimler V8-250 die Qualität . . . die Ausdauer . . . die Leistung . . . die Sicherheit und den Komfort, die jede Anforderung erfüllen.

## Chosen for Greatest Reliability . . everywhere

To the man who uses his car in all imaginable driving conditio every day, the Daimler V8-250 offers quality . . . durability . performance . . . safety and comfort that fulfill every demand.

## Geräumige Gepäcksunterbringung

Der Kofferraum des Daimler V8-250 fasst 380 Liter. Er wird nachts beleuchtet und hat einen eigenen Raum unter dem Kofferraumboden für Reserverad und Werkzeugbehälter.

## Spacious Luggage Storage

The luggage compartment of the Daimler V8-250 holds 380 liters. It lighted at night and has a separate well under the luggage space flo for the spare wheel and tool kit.

## A highly cultivated V8 power- plant

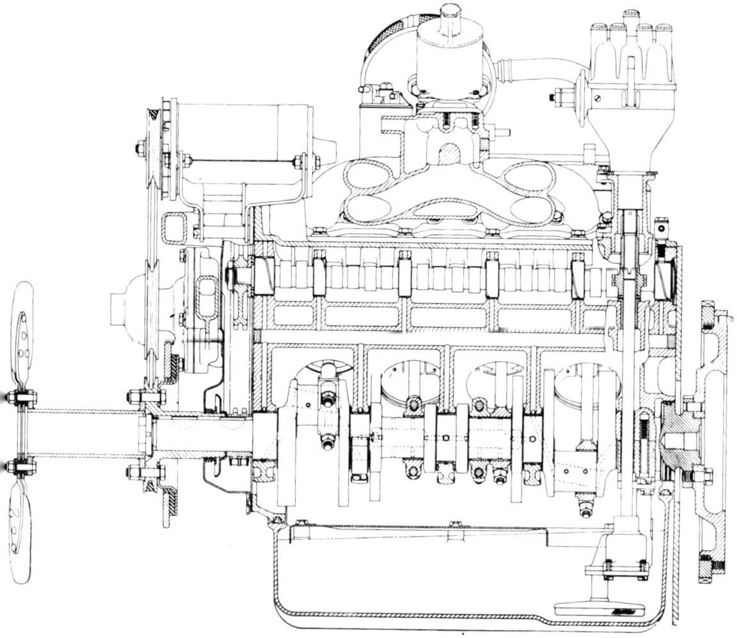

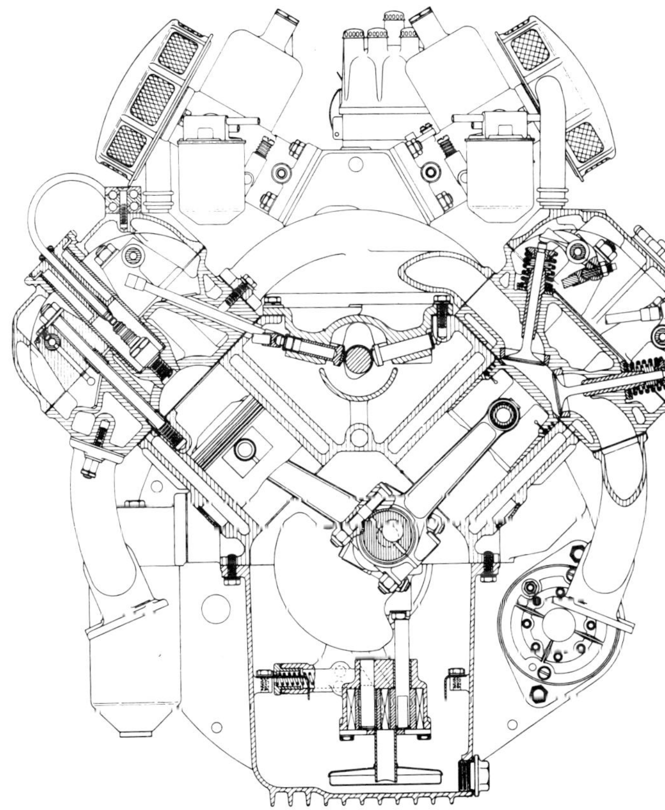

Left: A spare wheel under the floor of the luggage compartment may be advantageous in terms of economic utilization of space—but if one needs the wheel in the case of a flat, one has to unload all the luggage to get at it . . .

A splendid machine, the Daimler 2.5 liter eight-cylinder motor, with its short stroke and hemispherical combustion chambers. Two SU downdraft carburetors provided the powerplant with the necessary mixture of gasoline and air, and a central camshaft activated the valves via pushrods.

# Hauptabmessungen

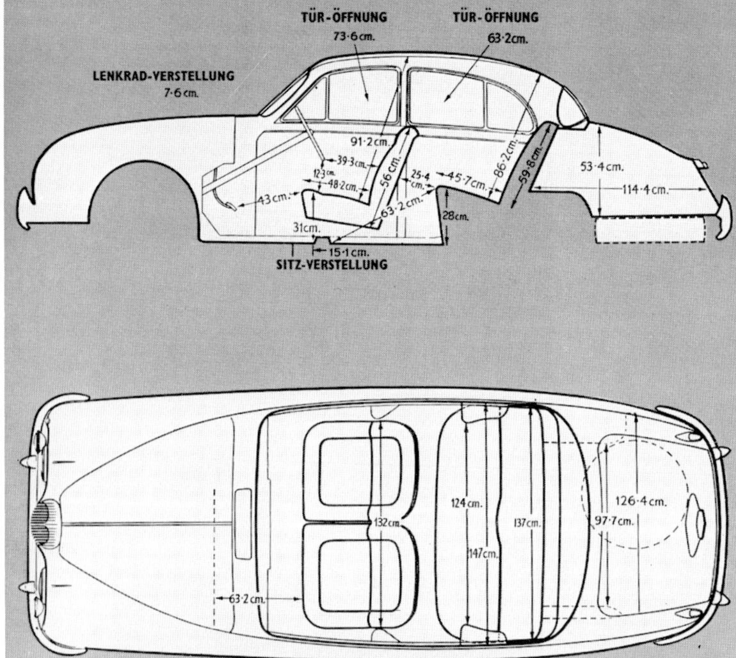


THE DAIMLER COMPANY LIMITED · COVENTRY · ENGLAND

*Diese Druckschrift ist nicht Bestandteil eines Angebotes. Änderungen der darin beschriebenen Ausstattung bei Lieferung in andere Länder bleibt vorbehalten. Die Daimler Company Ltd. behält sich das Recht vor, jederzeit Änderungen vorzunehmen, die von den in diesem Prospekt beschriebenen Angaben abweichen.*

# Farbschema

V8-250

Die nachstehend aufgeführten Farbkombinationen sind serienässig lieferbar. Jegliche Abweichung, wodurch Spezialbehandlung von Karosserie und/oder Polsterung erforderlich wird, muss zusätzlich berechnet werden. Angebot wird gern erteilt.

| Karosserie-Lackierung | Polsterfarben |
|---|---|
| CREME | ROT, HELLBLAU, DUNKELBLAU |
| BEIGE | ROT, WILDLEDERGRÜN, BRAUN, HELLBRAUN |
| WARWICK GRAU | ROT, DUNKELBLAU, HELLBRAUN |
| WEIDENGRÜN | WILDLEDERGRÜN, HELLBRAUN, BEIGE, GRAU |
| BRITISH RACING GREEN | WILDLEDERGRÜN, BEIGE, BRAUN, HELLBRAUN |
| DUNKELBLAU | ROT, HELLBLAU, GRAU |
| SCHWARZ | ROT, GRAU, BRAUN, HELLBRAUN |
| GOLDEN SAND | ROT, HELLBRAUN |
| OPALSILBERGRAU | ROT, HELLBLAU, DUNKELBLAU, GRAU |
| OPALSILBERBLAU | DUNKELBLAU, GRAU |
| OPALROTBRAUN | ROTBRAUN, BEIGE |

## Main Dimensions

**Door opening Door opening**
**Steering wheel adjustment 73.6 cm 63.2 cm**
**7.6 cm**
**15.1 cm**
**Seat adjustment**

This publication is not part of a sales offer. Changes of the therein described equipment are reserved for deliveries to other countries. The Daimler Company Ltd. reserves the right to make changes at any time that deviate from the data given in this brochure.

## Color Schemes

The color combinations listed below are available as standard. Any deviation which requires special handling of body and/or upholstery must be charged extra for. The cost will be stated gladly.

| Body color | Upholstery colors |
|---|---|
| Cream | Red, light blue, dark blue |
| Beige | Red, leather green, brown, light brown |
| Warwick gray | Red, dark blue, light brown |
| Meadow green | Leather green, light brown, beige, gray |
| British racing green | Leather green, beige, brown, light brow |
| Dark blue | Red, light blue, gray |
| Black | Red, gray brown, light brown |
| Golden sand | Red, light brown |
| Opal silver gray | Red, light blue, dark blue, gray |
| Opal silver blue | Dark blue, gray |
| Opal red-brown | Red-brown, beige |

**In its outer and inner dimensions, the Daimler 2.5 Liter corresponded exactly to the Mark II models. When in 1967 the Mark II types were called 240 and 340, the Daimler was also renamed V8 250, but its leather upholstery remained standard. Of note in the color chart: the typical color for sporting cars from England was "British Racing Green".**

# 1967-68

**The "S" models with 3.4 or 3.8 liter motors were slightly enlarged editions of the Mark II with the emphasis on refined furnishing and comfort.**

The fine line of JAGUAR vehicles known for their outstanding quality is even increased by the introduction of the 3.4 and 3.8 "S" models.

These compact "S" models include the newest developments and refinements in technology and design from the JAGUAR works.

With smooth body lines and spacious interior that offers comfortable seating to five people, plus independent front and rear suspension, disc brakes on all four wheels, new non-step heat and ventilation regulation, inclining seats, two independent fuel tanks, large luggage space and other typical characteristics, the "S" models carry on the traditional JAGUAR line, which exemplifies excellent performance, comfort and great retainment of value.

Das grosse Angebot der durch hervorragende Qualität und Leistung bekannten JAGUAR-Fahrzeuge wird durch das Erscheinen der 3.4 und 3.8 "S"-Modelle noch erweitert.

Diese kompakten "S"-Modelle stellen die neueste Entwicklung und Verfeinerung in Technik und Formgestaltung durch die JAGUAR-Werke dar.

Mit ausgewogener Karosserie und grosszügigem Innenraum, der fünf Personen bequem Platz bietet, sowie Einzelradaufhängung vorn und hinten, Scheibenbremsen an allen vier Rädern, neues stufenlos regulierbares Heizungs- und Belüftungssystem, Liegesitze, zwei unabhängige Benzintanks, grosser Koferraum und anderen charakteristischen Mermalen führen die "S"-Modelle die traditionelle JAGUAR-Linie fort, die ausgezeichnete Fahrleistung, Komfort und grosse Wertbeständigkeit vertritt.

## TECHNICAL DATA OF THE DAIMLER V8-250

**MOTOR:** 8-cylinder 90-degree V motor, 4 cylinders in each bank, bore 76.2 mm, stroke 69.85 mm, displacement 2548 cc, compression ratio 8.2:1, producing 140 HP at 5800 rpm. Dropped valves, single central camshaft with chain drive. 2 S.U. downdraft carburetors, type H.D. 6, with dual exhaust. Thermostatically regulated water-cooling. Circulation by pump. Pressure lubrication by oil pump with built-in mainstream filter. Cast iron cylinder block. Cylinder heads of special aluminum alloy with hemispherical combustion chambers, aluminum alloy pistons, steel connecting rods.

**TRANSMISSION:** *Fully synchronized mechanical:* Four-speed gearbox. Gearshift on the driveshaft tunnel in the center of the car. Gear ratios: first gear 13.00, second gear 8.42, third gear 5.66, fourth gear 4.27, reverse gear 14.95. "Borg and Beck" sprung diaphragm clutch. Universal joint with needle bearings. Hypoid differential. *With overdrive:* Same as above with a "Laycock-de Normanville" fast gear (overdrive) with control on the steering column. Gear ratios: first gear 13.85, second gear 8.98, third gear 6.04, fourth gear 4.55, overdrive 3.56, reverse gear 15.9.
**Automatic transmission:** Two drive sections. Automatic gear selector on steering column. Gear ratios: low 20.4 10.2, intermediate 12.38 6.19, top 8.54 4.27, reverse gear 17.85 8.92.

**SUSPENSION:** Independent front suspension with wishbone links and coil springs with telescopic shock absorbers. Rear suspension with semi-elliptic leaf springs with telescopic shock absorbers. Transverse stabilizer.

**BRAKES:** Servo-assisted disc brakes with quickly replaced brake pads. Automatically adjusting hand brake. Hand brake also activates the brake fluid warning light.

**STEERING:** Ball-joint steering with two-spoke steering wheel of 43.5 cm diameter. Steering column length adjustable. Choice of left- or right-hand drive. 4.7 revolutions from block to block. Turning circle 10.5 meters. Power steering optional.

**WHEELS AND TIRES:** Pressed steel disc wheels. Dunlop RS5 640 x 15 tires with tubes. Spare wheel with tire. Decorative hubcaps.

**FUEL SYSTEM:** By electric S.U. pump. Tank capacity 54 liters.

**ELECTRIC SYSTEM:** 12-volt Lucas battery, 51 amp std. 10 h norm with voltage regulator. A.C. generator. Side lamps with red warning lights in case bulbs fail, visible from driver's seat, set in front fenders. Foot switch for changing from high to low beams. Flasher switch on steering column. Two fog lights. Separate brake and taillights, directional and back-up lights mounted in one housing. Rear license plate light. Directional lights with automatic shutoff and indicator lights. Indirect lighting of the instruments and lettered control switches by two-stage switch. Map-reading light over the instrument panel. Interior lighting by two lights over the door pillars and one over the rear window, activated by a switch on the instrument panel as well as automatically by opening one of the four doors. Cigarette lighter with illuminated socket. Two dual-tone horns. Two windshield wipers, controllable at two speeds, with automatic return. Electric windshield washer system. Starter. Automatic ignition by pressure and current regulation. Oil coil. Speedometer (13 cm diameter), electric tachometer (13 cm diameter) with electric clock. Ammeter. Electric oil pressure gauge, water temperature gauge and fuel gauge with warning light. Combined warning light for brake fluid and hand brake.

**BODYWORK:** Four-door five-seat sedan with all-steel body. The self-supporting body offers highest rigidity at lightest weight. Large-surface windshield with slim pillars, bowed and electrically heated rear window guarantee best view to front and rear. The bowed windshield in no way interferes with getting in and out. Large non-glare adjustable rear-view mirror. Chromed window frames on all doors. Special door handles with built-in push buttons that do not freeze in even the coldest weather. Chromed ornamental strips along rain gutter and doors. Seats covered with finest "Vanmol" leather and upholstered with Dunlopillo foam rubber. The separate front seats are adjustable in height and distance. On the dashboard, which is made of polished walnut wood with padded edges, are tachometer and speedometer, directly in driver's field of vision; beside them are oil-pressure, water temperature and fuel gauges and ammeter. Locking glove compartment with interior light on the passenger's side. Space for installing radio and speaker. Two-spoke steering wheel with semicircular horn ring. All four doors have armrests and roomy pockets. Ashtrays on the back doors. Folding armrest in the middle of the back seat. Sun visors. Floor covered in velour carpet with thick felt underlay. Strong wraparound bumpers with overriders. Chromed door locks. Attachment points for front and rear seat belts.

**HEATER AND DEFROSTER:** High-performance heating system with windshield defroster. The fan is activated by a two-speed switch on the instrument panel.

**SPARE WHEEL AND TOOLS:** Spare wheel and tool kit are kept in an easily assessible well under the luggage compartment. Jack and lug wrench are in luggage compartment.

**JACKING THE CAR.** Jacking points to front and rear on both sides allow the car to be lifted easily by the supplied jack.

**MAIN DIMENSIONS:** Wheelbase 2.727 meters, front track 1.399 meters, rear track 1.355 meters, overall length 4.591 meters, overall width 1.460 meters, ground clearance 17.78 cm.

**The most noticeable body change compared to the Mark II: the lengthened trunk, which offered a definite plus in storage space. The well-known high-class atmosphere of all Jaguar cars prevailed in the interior.**

# JAGUAR

## „S"

**Elegante Reiselimousine**
**wahlweise mit 3,4 oder 3,8 l Motor**

**MOTOR:** Sechszylinder „XK"-Motor mit zwei obenliegenden um 70° versetzte Nockenwellen. Zwei Vergaser; Verdichtung 8 : 1.

**3,4 Liter:** Bohrung 83 mm × Hub 106 mm; Zylinderinhalt 3442 ccm; 210 PS bei 5500 U/min; 29,7 mkg bei 3000 U/min.

**3,8 Liter:** Bohrung 87 mm × Hub 106 mm; Zylinderinhalt 3781 ccm; 220 PS bei 5500 U/min; 33,1 mkg bei 3000 U/min.

**GETRIEBE:** Vollsynchronisiertes 4-Gang-Getriebe, Knüppelschaltung. Ein Schnellgang (Overdrive) kann durch einen Schalter an der Lenksäule zum vierten Gang zugeschaltet werden.
Gegen Aufpreis vollautomatisches Getriebe (Hydr. Drehmomentwandler und 3-Gang-Planetengetriebe). Wählhebel am Lenkrad.

**RADAUFHÄNGUNG:** Vorn Trapez-Dreieckquerlenker, Schraubenfedern, Teleskopstoßdämpfer und Torsionsstabilisator. Hinten Einzelradaufhängung mit gegabelten Führungsarmen, Halbachsen mit je zwei Universalgelenken und Längslenkern sowie je zwei Schraubenfedern mit innenliegenden Teleskopstoßdämpfern. Dies ist in einem leicht demontierbaren Hilfsrahmen zusammengefaßt, der durch Gummiaufhängungen mit der Karosserie verbunden ist.

**BREMSEN:** Vierradscheibenbremsen mit Bremshilfe, selbstnachstellend.
Handbremse, selbstnachstellend, wirkt mechanisch auf die Hinterräder.

**LENKUNG:** Kugelkreislauflenkung. Verstellbare Lenkradsäule.

**RÄDER UND BEREIFUNG:** 185×15 mit Schlauch. Gegen Aufpreis Speichenräder mit Zentralverschluß.

**KRAFTSTOFFVERSORGUNG:** Zwei elektrische Benzinpumpen. Zwei getrennte Tanks, vom Armaturenbrett aus umschaltbar. Tankinhalt 63 l.

**ELEKTRISCHE AUSRUSTUNG UND INSTRUMENTE:** 12-Volt-Anlage, Nebellampen, Rückfahrscheinwerfer, Scheibenwischer mit zwei Stufen, Scheibenwaschanlage, Lichthupe, Tourenzähler, Amperemeter, Uhr, Zigarrenanzünder etc.

**KAROSSERIE:** Selbsttragende Sicherheits-Karosserie, 4-türig, 5 Plätze, Lederpolsterung, Veloursteppiche, vorn und hinten ausklappbare Armlehnen; das Armaturenbrett ist aus poliertem feingemasertem Walnußholz; Kofferrauminhalt 530 Liter; Reserverad und Werkzeug befinden sich unter dem Kofferraumboden.

**HEIZUNG UND BELUFTUNG:** Frischluft-Heizungssystem für vorn und hinten mit zweistufigem Gebläse. Für die Vordersitze ist diese Anlage getrennt regulierbar.

**HAUPTABMESSUNGEN:** Radstand 273 cm, Spur vorn 141 cm, Spur hinten 137 cm, Länge 477 cm, Breite 170 cm, Höhe 138 cm, Wendekreis 10,2 m.

# JAGUAR

## "S"

Elegant Touring Sedan
with optional 3.4 or 3.8 liter motor

**MOTOR:** Six-cylinder XK motor with dual overhead camshafts at 70 degrees. Dual carburetors; compression ratio 8:1.

**3.3 Liter:** Bore 83 mm, stroke 106 mm, displacement 3442 cc, 210 HP at 5500 rpm, torque 29.7 mkg at 3000 rpm.

**3.8 Liter:** Bore 87 mm, stroke 106 mm, displacement 3781 cc, 220 HP at 5500 rpm, torque 33.1 mkg at 3000 rpm.

**TRANSMISSION:** Fully synchronized 4-speed gearbox. Stock shift. One fast gear (overdrive) can be engaged by a switch on the steering column. Optional fully automatic transmission (hydraulic torque converter and 3-gear planetary gearbox) at higher price. Selector lever on steering wheel.

**SUSPENSION:** Front wishbone links, coil springs, telescopic shock absorbers and torsion stabilizer. Individual rear suspension with forked leading arms, half-axles with two universal joints and longitudinal links each, plus two coil springs each with telescopic shock absorbers inside. This is enclosed in an easily demounted subframe which is attached to the body by rubber mounts.

**BRAKES:** Four-wheel disc brakes with servo assistance, self-adjusting. Hand brake, self-adjusting, works mechanically on the rear wheels.

**STEERING:** Ball-joint steering. Adjustable steering column.

**WHEELS AND TIRES:** 185 x 15 with tubes. Optional spoked wheels with central attachment.

**FUEL SYSTEM:** Two electric fuel pumps. Two separate tanks, switch on instrument panel. Tank capacity 63 liters.

**ELECTRIC SYSTEM AND INSTRUMENTS:** 12-volt system. Fog lights, back-up light, two-speed windshield wipers, windshield washing system, flashers, tachometer, ammeter, clock, cigarette lighter etc.

**BODYWORK:** Self-supporting body, 4 doors, 5 seats, leather upholstery, velour carpets, folding front and rear armrests; the instrument panel is made of polished fine-grain walnut wood; luggage compartment volume 530 liters; spare wheel and tools kept under the luggage compartment.

**HEATING AND VENTILATION:** Fresh-air heating system for front and rear with two-speed fan. System separately controllable for the front seats.

**MAIN DIMENSIONS:** Wheelbase 273 cm, front track 141 cm, rear track 137 cm, length 477 cm, width 170 cm, height 170 cm, turning circle 10.2 meters.

## A new concept in safe, comfortable and fast driving

**The lengthening of the Mark II body to the rear was not a stylistic gain for every taste. In the process the car had lost some of its original dynamism; the emphasis here was more on comfort than on sportiness.**

The strong, silent motor of the JAGUAR "S", its extraordinarily good roadholding and luxurious interior decor guarantee absolute comfort under any traveling or road conditions.
Outstanding workmanship completes the picture of this luxury vehicle, which is incomparable in its class.

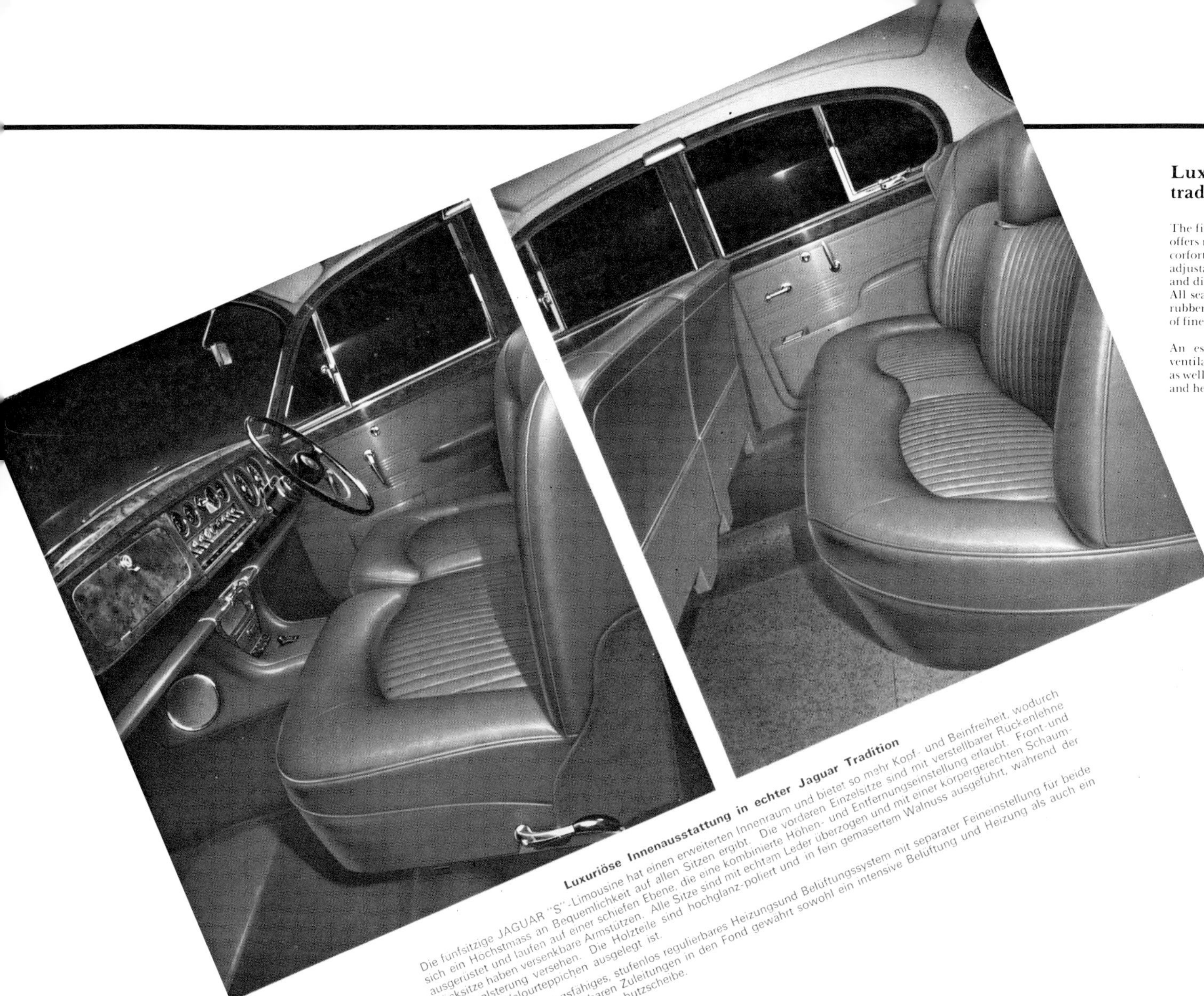

**Luxuriöse Innenausstattung in echter Jaguar Tradition**

Die fünfsitzige JAGUAR "S"-Limousine hat einen erweiterten Innenraum und bietet so mehr Kopf- und Beinfreiheit, wodurch sich ein Höchstmass an Bequemlichkeit auf allen Sitzen ergibt. Die vorderen Einzelsitze sind mit verstellbarer Rückenlehne ausgerüstet und laufen auf einer schiefen Ebene, die eine kombinierte Höhen- und Entfernungseinstellung erlaubt. Front-und Rücksitze haben versenkbare Armstützen. Alle Sitze sind mit echtem Leder überzogen und mit einer körpergerechten Schaum-gummipolsterung versehen. Die Holzteile sind hochglanz-poliert und in fein gemasertem Walnuss ausgeführt, während der Boden mit Velourteppichen ausgelegt ist.

Ein besonders leistungsfähiges, stufenlos regulierbares Heizungsund Belüftungssystem mit separater Feineinstellung für beide Frontsitze, sowie abschaltbaren Zuleitungen in den Fond gewährt sowohl ein intensive Belüftung und Heizung als auch ein direktes Entfrosten der Windschutzscheibe.

## Luxurious interior decor in true Jaguar tradition

The five-seat JAGUAR "S" sedan has an enlarged interior and thu offers more headroom and foot space, providing the highest degree o corfort in all seats. The individual front seats are equipped witl adjustable backs and move at an incline that allows a combined high and distance adjustment. Front and rear seats have folding armrests All seats are covered in genuine leather and upholstered with foan rubber for proper fit. The wooden parts are highly polished and mad of fine-grain walnut, while the floor is covered with velour carpeting

An especially high-performance, smoothly regulated heat anc ventilation system includes separate fine controls for both front seat as well as closing rear ducts, and guarantees both intensive ventilatior and heating and direct defrosting of the windshield.

**The interior space of the S models had also increased somewhat, so that nothing was lacking for comfortable travel, with generous use of leather and velour. The huge luggage space could hold luggage for five people.**

Der grosszügig gestaltete mit einer Innenbeleuchtung versehene Kofferraum hat ein Fassungsvermögen von ca. 532 Litern und ist zum Schutz der Gepäckstücke gepolstert. Zwecks müheloser Betätigung ist die Haube des Kofferraums mit Gegengewichten versehen.

Die reichhaltige Instrumentierung, zusammen mit den übersichtlich angeordneten Bedienungsschaltern, bildet einen Teil des in poliertem Walnussholz ausgeführten Armaturenbrettes. Für die persönlichen Sachen ist ein abschliessbarer Handschuhkasten vorhanden, der von innen beleuchtet ist. Unter dem Armaturenbrett verläuft in gesamter Breite ein Ablagefach.

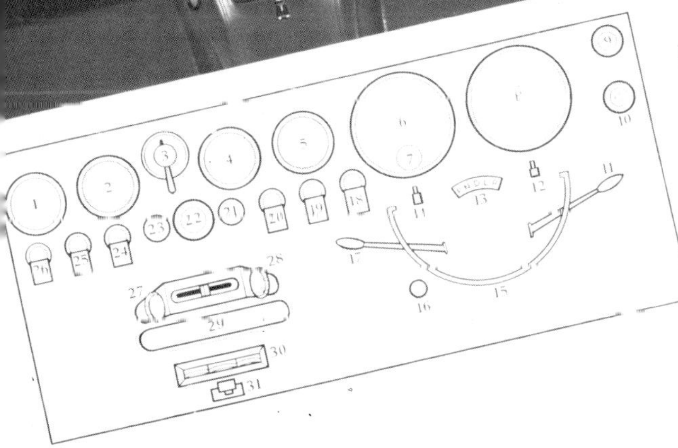

ANORDNUNG DER INSTRUMENTE UND BEDIENUNGSSCHALTER

1. Ampèremeter
2. Benzinuhr
3. Lichtschalter
4. Öldruckmesser
5. Wassertemperaturanzeiger
6. Drehzahlmesser
7. Elektrische Zeituhr
8. Geschwindigkeitsmesser
9. Schaltsperre (nur bei automatischem Getriebe)
10. Warnlicht für Bremsflüssigkeitsstand und Handbremse
11. Schalthebel für automatisches Getriebe
12. Tageskilometereinstellung
13. Schaltschema für automatisches Getriebe
14. Zeituhrverstellung
15. Hupenring
16. Abblendschalter
17. Fahrtrichtungsanzeiger und Lichthupe
18. Scheibenwaschanlage
19. Scheibenwischer
20. Benzintankumschalter
21. Starterknopf
22. Zigarettenanzünder
23. Zündschloss
24. Gebläse
25. Armaturenbrettbeleuchtung
26. Kombinierte Innen- und Kartenbeleuchtung
27. und 28. Getrennt regulierbare Heizungs- und Belüftungseinstellung für Vordersitze.
29. Platz für Radio
30. Heizungs- und Frischluftschalter
31. Schalter für Belüftung bzw. Heizung im Fond

Die Illustration zeigt das Modell mit Rechtslenkung, im Modell für Europa mit Linkslenkung sind die Instrument Einrichtungen entgegengesetzt arrangiert.

The large-dimension luggage compartment with interior lighting has a capacity of about 532 liters and is upholstered for the safety of the luggage. For easy lifting, the trunk lid is fitted with counterweights.

The generous array of instruments, along with the easy-to-see arrangement of the controls, forms one part of the polished walnut dashboard. A locking glove compartment for personal effects is available, with an interior light. Under the dashboard is a shelf running its entire length.

**ARRANGEMENT OF INSTRUMENTS AND CONTROL SWITCHES**

1. Ammeter
2. Fuel gauge
3. Light switch
4. Oil pressure gauge
5. Water temperature gauge
6. Tachometer
7. Electric clock
8. Speedometer
9. Automatic transmission lock
10. Warning light for brake fluid and hand brake
11. Automatic gear selector
12. Daily odometer
13. Automatic transmission switch
14. Clock setting control
15. Horn ring
16. Dimmer switch
17. Directional signal and flasher lever
18. Windshield washer control
19. Windshield wiper control
20. Fuel tank switch
21. Starter button
22. Cigarette lighter
23. Ignition lock
24. Fan switch
25. Dashboard light switch
26. Combined interior and map-reading light switch
27 & 28. Separate front seat heat and ventilation controls
29. Space for radio
30. Heat and fresh air control
31. Rear heat or ventilation control

The illustration shows the right-hand-drive model. In the left-hand-drive model made for Europe, the instruments are arranged in the opposite order.

**VORNE**

An Trapez-Dreieckquerlenkern,
Schraubenfedern und Teleskop-
stoss-dämpfern, sowie Kurven-
stabilisator. Diese Anordnung
ist zusammen mit dem Lenk-
gehäuse in einen Hilfsrahmen
montiert, der seinerseits mittels
Gummilagerungen an der Karo-
sserie befestigt ist.

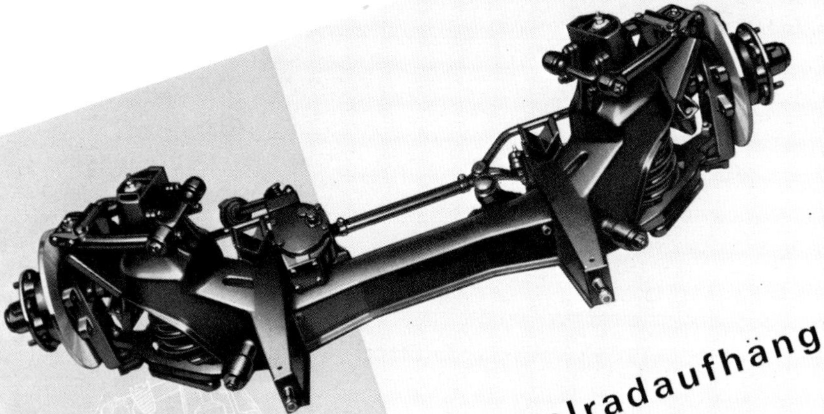

**Einzelradaufhängung . . . . .**

**HINTEN**

An untenliegenden, gegabelten
Führungsarmen und darüber-
liegenden Halbachsen mit
Universalgelenken,sowieLängs-
lenkern. Auf beiden Seiten je
zwei Schraubenfedern mit
Teleskopstossdämpfern. Innen-
liegende, am Differentialge-
hause befestigte Scheiben-
bremsen. Diese Anordnung ist
ebenfalls in einen Hilfsrahmen
montiert, der mittels Gummila-
gerungen an der Karosserie
befestigt ist.

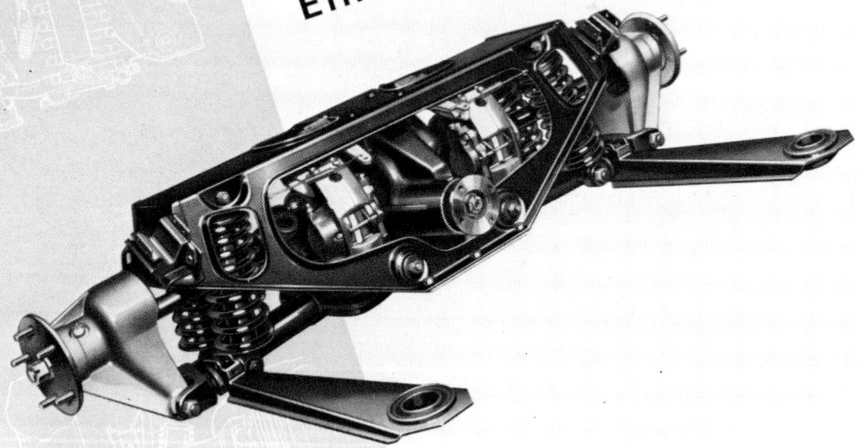

**FRONT**
Wishbone transverse links, coil springs and telescopic shoc absorbers, as well as curve stabilizer. This arrangement, alon with the steering system, is mounted in a subframe that in turn i attached to the body with rubber mounts.

**Independent Suspension...**

**REAR**
Forked bottom leading arms and half-axles with universal join above, as well as longitudinal links. Two coil springs wit telescopic shock absorbers inside on each side; disc brake attached to the differential housing. This arrangement likewise mounted in a subframe attached to the body with rubbe mounts.

**A well-built and well-tuned suspension guaranteed the travelers a non-tiring trip, even when the road conditions left something to be desired; the driver controlled either a four-speed transmission with overdrive or an automatic transmission, which basically was better suited to the characteristics of the S model, took over the job.**

# Hauptmerkmale des Jaguar 'S'

## Main characteristics of the Jaguar "S"

Comfortable five-seat sedan, luxuriously equipped and splendidly built.

Independent suspension, disc brakes on all four wheels. Individual front seats with combined distance and height adjustment, as well as adjustable seat backs and folding armrests.

Rear seats formed to fit the body, with central armrest, offer a maximum of comfort for two to three persons.

High-performance heating and ventilation system with no-step control.

Large luggage space with a capacity of circa 532 liters.

Choice of 3.4 or 3.8 liter motor.

Choice of fully synchronized four-speed transmission with fast gear (overdrive) or fully automatic transmission.

Two separate fuel tanks with a total capacity of 64 liters.

A wealth of instrumentation.

Whether a Daimler, Mark II or Type S, each of these cars incorporated in an impressively stylish way the "made in England" automobile culture, and every lucky owner of such a car today possesses a piece of automobile history.

JAGUAR "S"
Overall Dimensions

V8 250

# Jaguar Mark II in Miniature

| Manufacturer | Form | Material | Scale |
|---|---|---|---|
| **JAGUAR 2.4** | | | |
| Corgi Toys (GB) | Readymade | Diecast | 1/45 |
| Corgi Toys (GB) | Readymade Flywheel Motor | Diecast | 1/45 |
| Corgi Toys(GB) | Readymade Fire Chief | Diecast | 1/45 |
| Milton (India) | Readymade | Diecast | 1/45 |
| Revell (USA) | Kit | Plastic | 1/45 |
| Norev (F) | Readymade | Plastic | 1/43 |
| Minic (GB) | Readymade | Plastic | 1/36 |
| Startex (GB) | Readymade | Tinplate | 1/30 |
| Mettoy (GB) | Readymade | Plastic | 1/24 |
| Tri-ang (GB) | Readymade | Plastic | 1/24 (2 types) |
| Bandaiya (J) | Readymade | Tinplate | 1/20 (approx. scale) |
| Bandaiya (J) | Readymade | Tinplate | 1/20 Convertible |
| **JAGUAR 3.4 Mark I** | | | |
| Matchbox (GB) | Readymade | Diecast | 1/72 |
| Modsport (GB) | Kit | Metal | 1/72 |
| **JAGUAR 3.4 Mark II** | | | |
| Matchbox (GB) | Readymade | diecast | 1/72 |
| Minix (GB) | Readymade | Plastic | 1/72 |
| Classic 43 (GB) | Readymade | Metal | |
| Dinky Toys (GB) | Readymade | Diecast | 1/43 |
| Eligor (CH) | Readymade | Diecast | 1/43 |
| Eligor (CH) | Readymade | Diecast | 1/43 Tour de France |
| Eligor (CH) | Readymade | Diecast | 1/43 Police |
| Provence Moulage (F) | Kit | Plastic | 1/43 |
| Provence Moulage (F) | Kit | Plastic | 1/43 Workshop Car |
| Spot-On (GB) | Readymade | Diecast | 1/42 |
| Spot-On (GB) | Readymade | Diecast | 1/42 Police |
| Peetzy (D) | Readymade | Plastic | 1/40 |
| **JAGUAR S-TYPE** | | | |
| Spot-On (GB) | Readymade | Diecast | 1/42 |
| Modsport (GB) | Kit | Metal | 1/43 |

# The Jaguar Mark II in the Press

The name of Jaguar has long evoked a fascination that not even the motoring press has been able to avoid. They spoke of the "great independent" and the "big cat of Coventry", of "British nobility" and "perfection from tradition". To be sure, the factory itself was generous with superlatives, even though they were wrapped in respectability.

In December of 1957, *Auto, Motor und sport* spoke of a particular high-performance car that had been introduced in London two years before: "A comfortable touring car that can pull away effortlessly from most sports cars."

The 3.4 was added at that time: "The 2.4 Liter was constructed from the start so that the larger 3.4-liter motor fit under the hood—and from such a combination the 3.4 Liter has now arisen. While the smaller motor is limited to 112 HP by a comparatively small carburetor and intake capability in the interests of economy, the larger motor of the 3.4 Liter is used in its 210-HP version. The result is a car that, tested under remarkably bad weather conditions, reached a speed of 198 kph as an average of four measurements . . ."

The Jaguar was not at all to be regarded as a sports car, wrote Paul Frére, for it offered everything in convenience, comfort, quiet running and elasticity that a non-sporting driver could wish for. The car was also comparatively thrifty. At speeds around 125 kph in testing, the consumption did not amount to more than 12.5 liters per 100 kilometers, and using full power did not raise it over 16 liters (the model had overdrive).

"In fast gear (overdrive) the motor very rarely turns over 4000 rpm. At 130 the tachometer needle just reaches 3000, and at 200 it does not go over 4500. Only at 5000 rpm does the motor begin to get somewhat louder. And since it runs very softly at slower speeds too and gives good torque, the Jaguar can be driven almost exclusively in fourth gear on normal roads too, and can accelerate from 40 kph up as quickly as most touring cars in the most appropriate gear and easily surpass 185 kph before one has to shift to fast gear. The brakes meet the requirements of normal driving and—thanks to a vacuum servo—require only a little bit of power. . . . The sound damping is also particularly successful; in particular, the irritating drone of the body was almost completely eliminated." The passengers of a 3.4 Liter, said Paul Frère, could scarcely tell with their eyes closed whether they were riding on mediocre asphalt or a well-paved concrete road.

The English magazine *The Autocar* also spoke of a "Gran Turismo Saloon". "The biggest surprise in this comfortable car is the quick acceleration with only moderate fuel consumption." The Jaguar's interior lived up to the marque's standards: "The leather-covered seats, the highly-polished wood of the dashboard and window frames, as well as the thick carpets, are taken for granted in a Jaguar. The 3.4 Liter's standard equipment includes two speed windshield wipers, a windshield washing system, a cigarette lighter, a clock, heating and ventilation." Even before the 3.4 was officially introduced, *The Autocar* knew, the factory had shipped 200 cars to America in order to supply American dealers before the first press reports came out.

The Americans spoke of a real sensation when the 3.4 Liter arrived there. The 2.4 Liter had already been

Finished in a golden bronze—this Mark II is an individualist's collector car.

Above: Things also look good under the hood of the Mark II shown at left. First-class restoration without regard to cost . . .

well received in the States. "Here is a vehicle that not only looks wonderful and offers a lot of comfort, but in terms of performance leaves everything that comes from Detroit in its dust", as was written in *Autosport* in April of 1957. Quiet running, elasticity, and fine workmanship were praised—and again and again the amazing sports-car performance, thoroughly uncommon for a five-seat touring sedan. "This product from Coventry deserves to be among the most desirable automobiles—really a car to be loved!"

That the motor was not only powerful but also lovely to look at was attested to by Paul Frère: "The dual overhead cam motor is beautiful with its highly polished cam covers, carburetors, light-metal intake and water pipes and its black-enameled exhaust pipes. To be sure, the sidewalls come rather close to the motor, which does not exactly facilitate access to the components located beside the motor. Those that need regular service, though, are accessible enough,

**Recently offered for sale in Munich: a 1963 Daimler V8. It was not cheap!**

which is also true of the oil dipstick, though it must be added that in the dark it is much easier to take it out than to get it back in! Experience tells us that the thermo-electric SU starting carburetor makes the motor start quickly even in very cold weather. It is switched off automatically as soon as the water temperature has risen enough, which takes just a short time. In spite of that, one occasionally wishes for a manual choke.

"All in all, one may well say that the 3.4 Liter Jaguar is a car with an iron hand in a velvet glove, and there are few touring cars today that the sports-car fan can enjoy as much as the newest Jaguar."

The 2.4 Liter had already been described in *Autosport* as "the best all-round auto". This car was a milestone, it was said. "The machine is more elastic than any other comparable powerplant of its size. Even in overdrive one can get through the heaviest city traffic. One can really be lazy about shifting." *Road & Track:* "One could speak of a 'silent sports car', if only someone else hadn't already claimed this slogan." The reference was to Bentley.

Jaguar went into the 1959/60 model year with no fewer than ten basic models. And although the contemporary XK 150 was naturally the most desirable of all Jaguars, everybody talked about the new "Mark Two". Its styling was that of the 2.4/3.4, but a lot of technical refinements had turned the sedan into the "Nonplusultra of an automobile" *(Motor Age)*. And the car was also available with the powerful 220-HP 3.8 liter motor. The servo disc brakes front and rear also made a great impression.

"Who drives a Jaguar?" asked *Auto, Motor & Sport* in 1959, and gave the answer:

"Two things interest us: What kind of people drive a Jaguar, and how has this car gone over in Germany? So as not to dissipate our energy, we have chosen the Mark VIII to represent the marque. The first question was answered more quickly than the second.

"Because of the high tax on engine displacement in Germany—which is higher than in other countries—the market for cars above the 3-liter boundary is only a limited one. This means too that used Jaguars simply do not sell there. If their owners trade them in, usually for a newer type of Jaguar, they are generally sold to Americans.

"Around 150 "Marks" (VII and VIII) are running in Germany. Altogether there are about 420 Jaguars of all kinds and years in use there. About 70% of the Mark VIII are owned by Americans and Britons. The rest belong to well-known names in the world of business, and it is interesting to note how many business people there are who do not want to miss out on above-average driving experiences amid all their business travel. The "Marks" are often driven by chauffeurs, who are also responsible for the care and maintenance of them. Since their owners always have a second car, nothing prevents them from sending their Jaguars to a city, usually some distance away, where Jaguar service is available, when they need it. (There are Jaguar agencies in 13 German cities.) The reasonably-priced 3.4 Liter "sport sedan" sells best. It is usually driven with passion by devoted fans and sporting drivers themselves."

About a year later, the same magazine published a test report on the Mark II 3.8 Liter: "A member of the classic English school—the car is so English that one is tempted to drink tea in it . . ." With fine nuances of arrogance, this magazine, *Ams* reported that in that year "only 7500 Americans could buy a Jaguar"—a suggestion that this car is absolutely not a product for the masses. Its advantages—in brief—were its quietly running motor with high power reserve, strong disc brakes, great driving comfort on long high-speed trips, good instrumentation and exclusive equipment. The Mark II's disadvantages were listed as a less than perfect gear synchronization (long shifting times, first gear not synchronized at all), quickly fading brakes, and a too-small fuel tank. But: "Its lines—especially in side view—are a synthesis of understated elegance and daring dynamics." A pleasant feature was the enlargement of the Mark II's window areas compared to its forerunners, with slimmer pillars and better all-round visibility. Dieter Korp went on: "An automobile like the Jaguar Mark 2 should be driven with gloves on, not only because it is more appropriate to the quiet elegance of this car, but also because it is a car that wants to be held firmly. For whoever would want to drive it with spirit over a long stretch—and it tempts one to—will all too easily feel it in his hands, not that the car makes its driver nervous, but that it has to be steered through fast curves with manly strength. But the joy of driving it is great. Passing—as if from a standing start—makes an impression like no other European sedan. When one opens the gas tap, as one might say, this passing on short stretches is like jumping, which is immediately stopped, if necessary, by the strongly acting brakes. Whoever knows how to adjust to the particular qualities of this car that is very interesting in terms of its price too, experiences a feeling of superiority that is almost impossible to find otherwise in this price and size class. In many ways, the Jaguar still embodies a good bit of that era when cars were still recognizable as cars, especially in terms of the external "personality", the honesty of the instruments, the careful breaking-in of a new car and the necessary care and service. We feel that it would somehow be a shame if there were no such cars any more. It is a shame too that in this country such nerve-calming displacement is so expensive!"

How a Jaguar Mark II performs in everyday use was described by a long-time owner in *The Motor* in

1963. "Amazing what this car really offers for its price. To put the durability of the motor to a decisive test one must drive it much harder over a very long period of time than a normal motorist would. But a long lifetime also requires that one keep very strictly to the running-in instructions and look at the dipstick more often than usual during this time. In the beginning, too, I often noted a relatively high fuel consumption, but this passed when the car had covered its first 4000 miles."

Richard Bensted-Smith also reported sudden motor stalling, especially at traffic-light stops. He learned from this to service the SU carburetors regularly, as their valves always needed a drop of oil. In cold starts and short trips during which the motor had no chance to warm up there was frequent misfiring. "But one should not use a racehorse to haul coal . . ."

Whatever disadvantages the Mark II might have, wrote *Car and Driver* in 1964, one must forgive them of this car because its performance is so splendid, it looks so good and, last but not least, it is so reasonably priced. "Among all the good cars, the Mark II 3.8 Liter is the most reasonably priced. From the value-for-money aspect, the Jaguar holds a strong position."

**Jaguar 3.8 Liter, made in 1962.**

# Technical Data for Comparison

| Model | Displacement cc | Bore x stroke | HP at rpm | Compression | Top speed | Number RHD | Number LHD | |
|---|---|---|---|---|---|---|---|---|
| MK 1 2.4 | 2483 | 83 x 76,5 | 112/5750 | 8:1 | 19,5 mKg | ca. 165 | 16250 | 3742 |
| MK 1 3.4 | 3442 | 83 x 106 | 162/5200 | 8:1 | 28,4 mKg | ca. 190 | 8945 | 8460 |
| MK 2 2.4 | 2483 | 83 x 76,5 | 120/5750 | 8:1 | 19,8 mKg | ca. 175 | 21768 | 3405 |
| MK 2 3.4 | 3442 | 83 x 106 | 162/5500 | 8:1 | 29,7 mKg | ca. 200 | 22095 | 6571 |
| MK 2 3.8 | 3781 | 87 x 106 | 168/5500 | 8:1 | 33,2 mKg | ca. 200 | 15383 | 14758 |
| 240 | 2483 | 83 x 76,5 | 133/5500 | 8:1 | 22,4 mKg | ca. 180 | 3716 | 730 |
| 340 | 3442 | 83 x 106 | 165/5500 | 8:1 | 29,7 mKg | ca. 200 | 2265 | 535 |
| Daimler 2.5 V8 | 2548 | 76,2 x 69,85 | 140/5500 | 8,2:1 | 19,4 mKg | ca. 180 | 3376 | 621 |
| Daimler 250 V8 | 2548 | 76,2 x 69,85 | 140/5500 | 8,2:1 | 19,4 mKg | ca. 180 | 4779 | 104 |

**Production was interrupted for only one day when in 1957 one third of the Jaguar factory was destroyed by fire . . .**

# Phases of Development of the Mark II/Daimler V8 1955-1969

1955
Introduction of the 2.4 Liter ("Mark I") in September.

1957
Introduction of the 3.4 Liter with wider grille in March. Rear-wheel spats with larger cutout, double exhaust pipes. Disc brakes optional. In the autumn all models were given the wider grille and different air cleaners.

1959
In January, new spoked wheels with 72 spokes instead of 60, electronic tachometer; in August, better ventilation under the windshield of the 2.4 Liter. In September, end of "Mark I" 2.4 and 3.4 liter production. In October, introduction of the Mark II 2.4, 3.4 and 3.8 with considerably modified bodywork, side lamps, windows enlarged all around, narrower pillars, new rear end with rear track 8 cm wider. Instruments now in front of the driver, brake indicator light, 2-spoke steering wheel, lie-down seats optional, heater and disc brakes standard.

1960
Servo steering standard. In May paper instead of oil-bath filter for 3.4 and 3.8 Liter. Opening of an assembly plant in South Africa.

1961
In February, torsion bar stabilizers, new sheath for oil dipstick. In June, stronger oil pumps. In August, self-adjusting hand brake. In December, new crankcase ventilation.

1962
In September, new piston rings. In November, introduction of the Daimler 2.5 Liter.

1965
From September on, first gear synchronized, clutch strengthened.

1966
From September on, imitation leather seat covers standard, genuine leather only optional.

1967
In June, new trunk lock, in August, new Varamatic servo steering, end of Daimler 2.5 Liter production. Introduction of the Daimler 250 V8. In September, end of Mark II 2.4, 3.4 and 3.8 Liter production. Introduction of Types 240 and 340 with slimmer bumpers, new ornamental grille style.

1968
End of 340 production in September

1969
End of 240 production in April, last Daimler 250 V8 leaves the factory in August.

BY APPOINTMENT TO
H.M. QUEEN ELIZABETH THE QUEEN MOTHER
MOTOR CAR MANUFACTURERS
JAGUAR CARS LIMITED

# Jaguar Clubs

**Jaguar Mark I/Mark II Register**
Thomas J. Muhs, Rebhalde 5, D 7133 Maulbronn, West Germany
**Jaguar S-Type/Mark X/420 Register**
Alfred Veninga, Grüne Strasse 6, D 3073 Liebenau, West Germany
**Jaguar Association Germany e.V.**
Club HQ: Poststrasse 369, D 2844 Lemfo''rde, West Germany
**Jaguar Drivers' Club Austria**
per Adr. DDr. Manfred Brandl, P.O. Box 19, A 4221 Steyregg, Austria
**Jaguar Drivers' Club**
The Norfolk Hotel, Harrington Road, London SW7, England
**Jaguar Drivers' Club Belgium**
30 Chemin des Deux Maisons, B 1200 Brussels, Belgium
**Jaguar Drivers' Club Switzerland**
Rudolf Luenenberger, P.O. Box 246, CH 3000 Bern 8, Switzerland
**Svenska Jaguar-Klubben**
Fack 42092, S 126 12 Stockholm, Sweden
**Jaguar Club Australia**
P.O. Box 161, Ringwood 3134, Australia
**Jaguar Club Wallis**
Dr. Imesch, 25 Ave, de la Gare, CH 1950 Sion, Switzerland
**Jaguar Daimler Club**
L. J. Meida, Kampiruysenstraat 64, NL 7552 NJ Hengelo, The Netherlands
**Jaguar Drivers' Club France**
39 Ave. de Laumière, F 75019 Paris, France

# Books for Jaguar Fans

**The Jaguar Tradition** by Michael Frostick. A guide to all Jaguar production models and racing cars from the beginning to 1973. An excellent illustrated volume from the house of Dalton Watson, for information and identification. 212 pages, more than 390 photos, English text.
**Jaguar—The Definitive History of a Great Car** by Andrew Whyte, with a foreword by Sir William Lyons. Precise descriptions and production figures for every model to 1980, including prototypes from prewar and racing cars from postwar times. 248 pages, 150 photos, English text.
**Jaguar Color Library.** This illustrated volume, in color throughout, from the house of Exeter treats the Jaguar brand. 48 pages, 126 color photos, English text.
**Jaguar: the Complete Illustrated History** by Philip Porter. An inclusive biography of the marque, with all passenger and sports cars into the Eighties. 160 pages, 330 b/w photos, 16 color pages, English text.
**Jaguar** by Lord Montagu. The fourth expanded edition, covering through the early Eighties, is an excellent book on the marque, with much information on the firm and the vehicles. 240 pages, 205 illustrations, English text.
**Jaguar—Great Marques** by Chris Harvey, with a foreword by Stirling Moss. After the three volumes on Ferrari, Mercedes and Porsche came this lovely illustrated book on the Jaguar marque. 80 pages, 85 illustrations, 79 of them in color, English text.

**Jaguar Super Profiles.** In this English series the authors give a detailed look at the problems of a single collector car. Reprints from contemporary periodicals, original factory publications, addresses of clubs and agencies finish the picture. The volume on Jaguar Mark II 2.4, 3.4 and 3.8 Liter sedans is of interest here. 56 pages, 20 color, 110 b/w photos, English text.

**Jaguar Cars** by R. M. Clarke. In the Brooklands Series, a number of volumes on the Jaguar marque have appeared. These reprints from contemporary publications offer an inclusive and deep look at the history and technology of these models; Jaguar Cars 1957-1961, Jaguar Cars 1961-1964. Each volume A4, approx. 100 pages, English text.

**Jaguar** by Lord Montagu of Beaulieu. This book in the Minimarque Series gives a good look at the development of these famous British cars. 159 pages, 127 illustrations, English text.

**Jaguar Pocket History** by Michael Frostick. A small volume introducing the Jaguar marque. 68 pages, 85 illustrations, 4 in color, English text.

**Jaguar Collector's Guide** by Paul Skilleter. In this series four volumes on Jaguars have already appeared, offering a wealth of technical and historical information for the enthusiast. Of interest here: The Jaguar Saloons. 128 pages, approx. 150 illustrations, English text.

**Jaguar for the Road** by Henry Rasmussen. In this renowned series a splendid volume on Jaguar has finally appeared. The models shown are: SS 100, XK 120 Roadster, XK 140 Drophead Coupe, XK 150 Coupe, Mark IX Sedan, Mark II Sedan, D-Type, E-Type I Roadster, E-Type II Coupe, E-Type III Roadster, XJ6 Sedan and XJ12. 300 illustrations, 120 in color, English text.

**Jaguar Saloon Cars** by Paul Skilleter. One of the best Jaguar experts has written this book, a companion to Jaguar Sports Cars. The two volumes together provide a thorough look at the Jaguar marque. 602 pages, 400 b/w and 25 color photos, English text.

**Jaguar—Great Marques Poster Book.** In this new companion series to the above one finds besides a short history of the firm the most important models of the marque with all data and outstanding photos. The individual photo pages can also be framed. 48 pages, 24 color photos, English text.

**Illustrated Jaguar Buyer's Guide** by J. Hoehn. A guidebook for all collectors and friends of this marque. 156 pages, 150 illustrations, English text. Out of print.

**Jaguar Since 1945** by Richard L. Busenkell. This book deals with the postwar Jaguar automobiles. Complete development of each model, many technical details, good illustrations. 152 pages, 142 b/w photos and 2 diagrams, English text. Out of print.

**Jaguar Brief Assembly Manual 1960-1970.** Reprint of the original in German. A4, WK 961.

**Jaguar 240 4-door 120 HP 2.5 L.** Reprint of the service manual in German, approx. 75 pages. A4, WK 960.

**Jaguar 340.** Reprint of the works manual. WK 1570.

**Jaguar 420G 4.2 Liter1974.** Reprint of the works manual. WK 1343.

**Jaguar 420 1967 Edition.** Spare parts list. J39.

**Jaguar 420 of 1972.** Workshop handbook. BL E143/2/

**Jaguar 420 1972 Edition.** Driver's manual. E137/4.

**Jaguar 2.4 L.** Reprint of the works manual in German. Approx. 70 pages, A4, WK 507.

**Jaguar 2.4 Mark 2 & 240, 1969 Edition.** Spare parts list. J33.

**Jaguar 3.4/3.8 L S.** Reprint of the works manual in German, approx. 90 pages. A4, WK 506.

**Jaguar Type 3.4 S/3.8 S.** Reprint of the assembly manual in German. Approx. 500 pages, A4, WK 1340.

**Jaguar 3.5 L Mark 7.** Reprint of the works manual, approx. 70 pages. A4, WK 508.

**Jaguar Daimler 6.** Driver's manual. Original British Leyland in German. AKM 048.

**Jaguar Mark 1, Mark 2 plus 240 & 340 Saloon 1955-1969.** Haynes repair manual. No. 098, English.

**Jaguar Mark 1, Mark 2 plus 240 & 240 Saloon 1955-1969.** Autobooks repair manual. No. 795, English text. Out of print.

**Jaguar Mark 2.** Original British Leyland works manual in English. Out of print.

**Jaguar Mark 7.** Spare parts list. J 21.

**Jaguar Mark 9.** Addenda to works manual of Mark 7, BL.